10 Minute Guide to ActiveX Control Pad

by Matthew E. Brown

A Division of Macmillan Computer Publishing
201 West 103rd St., Indianapolis, Indiana 46290 USA

This book is dedicated to the little jumpin' jumpin' guy that gave me inspiration on many late nights.

International Standard Book Number: 0-7897-1070-6
Library of Congress Catalog Card Number: 96-72217

99 98 97 4 3 2 1

Interpretation of the printing code: the rightmost double-digit number is the year of the book's printing; the rightmost single-digit number, the number of the book's printing. For example, a printing code of 97-1 shows that the first printing of the book occurred in 1997.

Screen reproductions in this book were created using Collage Plus from Inner Media, Inc., Hollis, NH.

President Roland Elgey

Publisher Joseph B. Wikert

Publishing Manager Jim Minatel

Title Manager Mark Cierzniak

Editorial Services Director Elizabeth Keaffaber

Managing Editor Sandy Doell

Director of Marketing Lynn E. Zingraf

Acquistions Manager Cheryl D. Willoughby

Acquistions Editor Jane K. Brownlow

Production Director Jon Steever

Production Editor Patricia Kinyon
Editors Sean Dixon, Patrick Kanouse, and Tonya Maddox
Product Marketing Manager Kristine Ankney
Assistant Product Marketing Managers Karen Hagen and Christy M. Miller
Strategic Marketing Manager Barry Pruett
Technical Editors Andy Angrick and Jim O'Donnell
Technical Support Specialist Nadeem Muhammed
Software Relations Coordinator Susan D. Gallagher
Editorial Assistants Jennifer L. Condon and Andrea Duvall
Book Designer Glenn Larsen
Cover Designer Dan Armstrong
Production Team Maureen Hanrahan, Malinda Kuhn, Daniela Raderstorf, Rowena Rappaport, and Christy Wagner
Indexer Bront Davis

About the Author

Matthew Brown lives in the small town of Addison, TX with his fiancée Caroline, and their children Ramses, Cleo, and Bastian. Matthew currently works at National Knowledge Networks, Inc. as the Webmaster and local Windows NT expert. In his free time, Matthew enjoys listening to music, go-cart racing, and watching mindless television for hours.

Contents

Introducing ActiveX Control Pad

The Internet is a quickly changing medium. Knowing that, you must realize that keeping up with all of the changes on the Internet is nearly impossible. By using *10 Minute Guide to ActiveX Control Pad* effectively, however, you will be that much ahead of other HTML authors and Web programmers active today.

With the introduction of the ActiveX Control Pad, Microsoft has bridged the gap between authoring static HTML documents and authoring complex Internet multimedia applications. This new authoring tool not only is accessible to the experienced programmer but is also approachable by someone with no programming experience at all. Through the use of easy to navigate menus, toolbars, and wizards, Microsoft has created a product that makes everyone successful at creating complex Web pages with only a few new features and technologies to learn.

What Is ActiveX Control Pad?

ActiveX Control Pad, simply defined, is a fully functional HTML authoring tool and ActiveX programming interface. Not only can you create dynamic HTML documents, but you can also control the exact layout of graphics and ActiveX controls.

What is HTML? Hypertext Markup Language is used on the Internet to create documents that are displayed in a Web browser. These files are simple text documents and saved as a *.htm or *.html file. You can use any text editor to create HTML files, even your favorite word processor. For more information about authoring with HTML, open your Web browser to **http://www.microsoft.com/workshop/author/newhtml/default.htm**.

Users that view your ActiveX-enabled Web pages need to use Internet Explorer 3.0 or Netscape Navigator 3.0 with the ScriptActive plug-in from NCompass Labs, located at **http://www.ncompasslabs.com/products/scriptactive.htm**. The reason for the limited choice of ActiveX-receptive browsers is that ActiveX technologies are so new. That fact should not detour you from writing HTML documents with ActiveX controls however. ActiveX controls have literally been around for years. They were formerly known as OLE (Object Linking and Embedding) components, used in Windows programming environments such as Visual Basic and Visual C++.

There are hundreds of ActiveX controls available on the Internet today. Many of these controls can be downloaded from Microsoft's Site Builder Network at **http://www.microsoft.com/activex/gallery/**. The controls explained in the lessons in this book, however, are those that ship with Internet Explorer 3.0 itself, so you do not need to download any further controls for this book to be useful.

What is Internet Explorer? Internet Explorer is a Web browser that allows you to navigate between HTML pages on the Internet. The program is freely downloadable from Microsoft's Web site, and you must have it installed for ActiveX Control Pad to function. If you do not have the browser, you will find it at **http://www.microsoft.com/ie**.

How to Use This Book Effectively

This book is organized into nineteen lessons which, when read in order, allow even the most novice HTML author to get quickly up to speed with ActiveX Controls and HTML Layout. These lessons are in order from least complex to most complex with the first few chapters introducing the new technologies slowly and in-depth. The latter chapters deal with the ActiveX controls themselves and how to use specific controls within your HTML documents.

What is HTML Layout? The ActiveX Control Pad allows you to develop special pages for use in your Web site called HTML Layout pages. HTML Layout allows you to place graphics and other objects in your Web page exactly as you want them to look when displayed. Many Web authors battled their way through tedious HTML code to get their graphics to display correctly before the release of HTML Layout with Internet Explorer 3.0

If you feel that skipping around to lessons that directly effect you suits your needs, feel free to do so. This book was designed to help you get up to speed with ActiveX controls quickly, and the author realizes that some readers are more familiar with the technology than others.

Each lesson in this book should take about 10 minutes to complete. Some may take a little more, some may take a little less. Many of the examples in this book are open ended, allowing you to experiment with your own design techniques and create hybrid applications from the examples. It would take hundreds, if not thousands, of pages in a book to fully describe ActiveX technologies and the ActiveX Control Pad. This book merely serves as a quick introduction to the information that you need right now.

For more in-depth analysis of the ActiveX Control Pad and ActiveX technologies, you might try another of Que's books such as *SE Using ActiveX*.

WHO NEEDS THIS BOOK

Perhaps you are a beginning HTML author or an experienced Windows programmer. Whatever your experience level with authoring Internet documents and programming with ActiveX controls, this book is for you.

Since the lessons each take about 10 minutes to complete, readers of all levels can quickly get up to speed with the new ActiveX technologies. Though you may not have a lot of time to devote to learning these new technologies, this book helps you develop your resources quickly and more effectively by cutting through the mindless chatter that many computer books contain and delving right into the information you are looking for.

CONVENTIONS USED IN THIS BOOK

You will notice that this book contains some special icons that you may not be familiar with (unless you have read other *10 Minute Guides*). The three icons are:

Panic Button You come across the Panic Button icon when you reach a critical point in the lesson where questions may come up or when an unexpected situation occurs. Though the author cannot guess every question that will arise, the effort is made to catch the most common questions. Here you will gain insightful answers to the questions that may arise.

Plain English This section appears when the technology lingo might be getting a little heavy. Many books delve into new vocabulary without providing definitions on what the author is talking about. This section attempts to explain a complex term or phrase by using plain English to fully define what is meant.

Timesaver Tips Timesaver Tips are just what the doctor ordered. These tips help introduce you to shortcuts or streamlined alternatives to the normal way of going about a procedure. Many times these consist of keyboard shortcuts or other ways of reducing the amount of time that it takes to complete a task.

You will also notice that some text is formatted differently than other. The following is a list of text conventions used in this book:

Italic	Signifies the introduction of a new term
Alt+Enter	Denotes pressing the Alt key in conjunction with the Enter key
`Monospace`	Indicates lines of code in sample applications
Bold	Text that should be typed by the user. Also indicates Web addresses
➥	Indicates continuation of the previous line of code

TRADEMARKS

ACKNOWLEDGMENTS

I would like to thank the Microsoft Corporation exclusively for pre-release versions of the ActiveX Control Pad and the associated documentation that goes with the program. Without the support of the Microsoft Web site, and their dedicated team of engineers, this book would have never been possible.

Many thanks must go to Jane Brownlow also who pushed me to write, even when there was no brain power on such late nights.

WE'D LIKE TO HEAR FROM YOU!

As part of our continuing effort to produce books of the highest possible quality, Que would like to hear your comments. To stay competitive, we *really* want you, as a computer book reader and user, to let us know what you like or dislike most about this book or other Que products.

You can mail comments, ideas, or suggestions for improving future editions to the address below, or send us a fax at (317) 581-4663. For the online inclined, Macmillan Computer Publishing has a forum on CompuServe (type **GO QUEBOOKS** at any prompt) through which our staff and authors are available for questions and comments. The address of our Internet site is **http://www.mcp.com** (World Wide Web).

In addition to exploring our forum, please feel free to contact me personally to discuss your opinions of this book: I'm **jsteever@que.mcp.com** on the Internet.

Thanks in advance—your comments will help us to continue publishing the best books available on computer topics in today's market.

Jon Steever
Que Corporation
201 W. 103rd Street
Indianapolis, Indiana 46290
USA

Although we cannot provide general technical support, we're happy to help you resolve problems you encounter that are related to our books, disks, or other products. If you need such assistance, please contact our Tech Support department at (800) 545-5914, ext. 3833.

To order other Que or Macmillan Computer Publishing books or products, please call our Customer Service department at (800) 835-3202, ext. 666.

ACQUIRING AND INSTALLING ACTIVEX CONTROL PAD

In this lesson, you learn how to download and install the ActiveX Control Pad.

AVAILABILITY OF THE ACTIVEX CONTROL PAD

Microsoft Corporation knows that if it is to stay successful in the Internet development market, it is going to have to get developers to use their products and technologies. To do this, Microsoft takes an approach similar to many other Internet-related companies, giving away the necessary tools to developers in the hope that new technologies, such as ActiveX controls and VBScript, will become standards among Web sites.

The ActiveX Control Pad is freely downloadable from Microsoft's Web site. Once Control Pad is downloaded and installed, you will have new resources, such as the Control Pad itself, a VBScript and JavaScript Wizard, and a graphical HTML Layout feature for creating sites exactly as you want them to look, to build active Web sites.

VBScript and JavaScript You can extend the use of ActiveX controls by including scripts within your HTML documents to further enhance the functionality of the controls themselves. Scripting languages, such as VBScript and JavaScript, provide a way to easily control how an ActiveX control functions and appears.

Before you begin downloading Control Pad, however, there are a couple of requirements:

- You must have either Windows 95 or Windows NT 4.0 installed. The ActiveX Control Pad cannot work with previous versions of Windows.
- You must install the newest official release of Internet Explorer, currently 3.1, available at **http://www.microsoft.com/ie/ie.htm**.

Once these requirements are met, you are ready to download and install the ActiveX Control Pad.

DOWNLOADING THE ACTIVEX CONTROL PAD

The ActiveX Control Pad is available as a single-file download from Microsoft's Web site. The file size is currently 2.7M and takes approximately 15 minutes to a half hour to download, depending on the speed of your Internet connection.

To begin downloading the Control Pad, follow these steps:

1. Initiate your connection to the Internet and launch Internet Explorer 3.0.
2. Choose File, Open, or alternatively, Ctrl+O. The Open dialog box appears.
3. Type **http://www.microsoft.com/workshop/author/cpad/** into the Open window and click OK. The ActiveX Control Pad site opens in your Web browser. Figure 1.1 shows the ActiveX Control Pad Web site as it will appear on your screen.

The ActiveX Control Pad home page is a framed site that is actually a portion of Microsoft's Site Builder Network. This Web site was set up to provide Web authors with up-to-the-minute guides to building Web sites with Microsoft tools and technologies. The left frame is a guide, containing tutorials and example sites to spawn new ideas, that helps you when you are authoring your Web content. The right frame is the ActiveX Control Pad Web page itself. From here, not only can you download Control Pad, but you can also read tutorials and gain valuable programming tips regarding ActiveX controls.

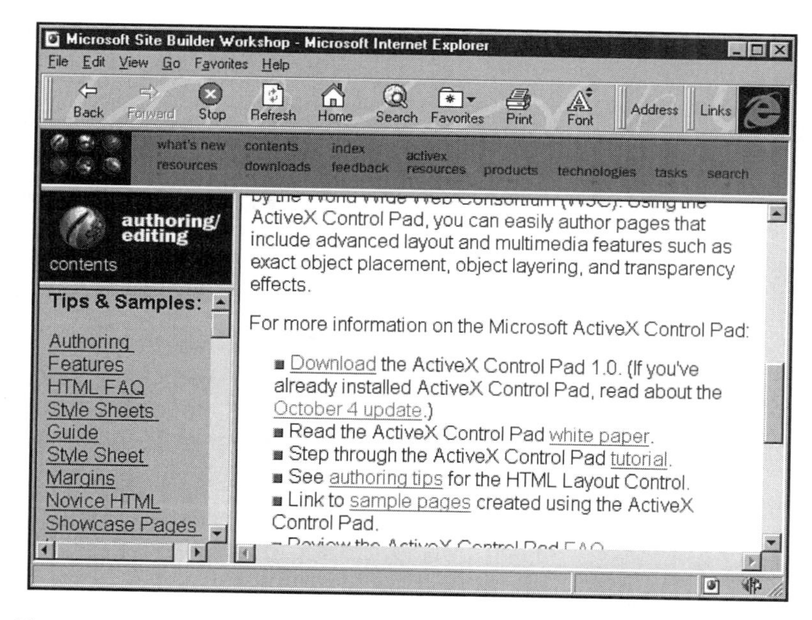

FIGURE 1. 1 The ActiveX Control Pad Web site is a great resource not only for downloading software but also as a technical reference.

Do I have enough free disk space? You will need about 3MB free on your hard drive to install the Control Pad. Also, keep in mind that you can free up about 3MB of disk space by deleting the compressed file (Setuppad.exe) after the installation.

To begin the download process, follow these simple steps:

1. Click the Download link. Your browser will open an Installation overview page allowing you to read further instructions before actually downloading the program file.
2. Click the `Download` hyperlink within the Web page. The compressed file, Setuppad.exe, begins downloading to your computer.
3. Click the Save to Disk button when prompted. Click OK. When prompted, choose a directory on your hard drive to save the file into and eventually install from. Figure 1.2 illustrates how the download process will look on your computer.

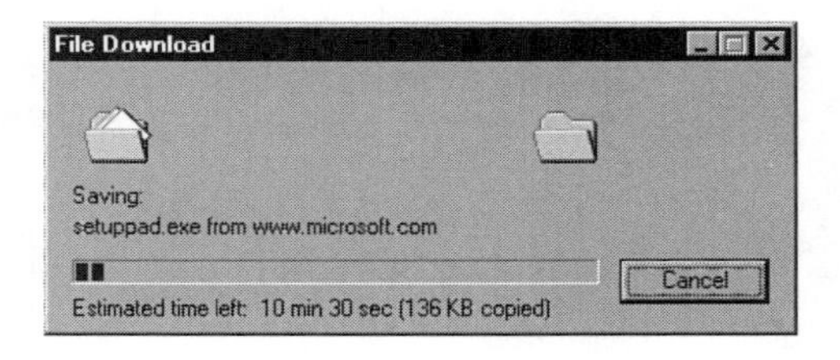

FIGURE 1.2 Downloading the ActiveX Control Pad is a simple process, although it will take some time to receive it fully on your computer.

Saving Files Quickly If you are using Internet Explorer to download the ActiveX Control Pad, you can hold down the Shift key while clicking a hyperlink to automatically begin downloading a file. You will still be prompted to save the file or open it as if you clicked the link normally.

Once the download process is complete, will be presented with a security dialog box confirming that you wish to save this file to your computer. Click OK to save the file. If you click Cancel, your time spent downloading will have been wasted. Now that the file is saved to your hard drive you are almost ready to begin the installation process. Before you install Control Pad, however, make sure that you add a link to your Favorites menu by pressing Ctrl+F to open the Favorites and Ctrl+A to save the site. The ActiveX Control Pad Web site is often updated with new information and new releases as they appear.

Installing the ActiveX Control Pad

If you have downloaded and installed other Microsoft software from the Internet, then you are already familiar with Microsoft's installation routines. Once the installation process is initiated, the only options that you are presented with are the Licensing Agreement for the software and the intended install directory.

To begin installing the ActiveX Control Pad, follow these steps:

1. Close any other programs that you might have currently running.
2. Open Windows Explorer by choosing Start, Programs, Windows Explorer from the Toolbar. Alternatively, you can double-click the icon titled Setuppad.exe that appeared in a window in the upper-left corner of your screen when the download process completed.
3. Locate the directory to which you downloaded the Setuppad.exe file. If you cannot locate the file, choose Tools (Ctrl+T), Find (Ctrl+F), Files or Folders (Ctrl+F) and search for the file.
4. Double-click Setuppad.exe to begin the installation process.

The first item that you are presented with upon beginning the installation is the End User License Agreement. You must read this agreement and consent to its terms before the installation process can continue. Click OK in the dialog box after reviewing the License Agreement. Figure 1.3 shows the License Agreement that will appear before you can continue with the installation.

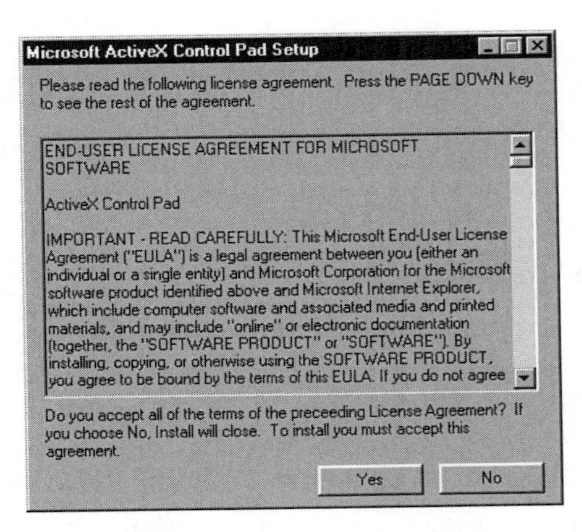

FIGURE 1.3 Before you can install the ActiveX Control Pad fully, you must read and agree to the terms in the License Agreement.

A dialog box will appear as the installer program extracts files and loads the ActiveX Control Pad Setup screen. When prompted, choose Continue (Ctrl+C) at the Setup screen. The installer does a quick search of your hard drive and tries to locate any other versions of the ActiveX Control Pad. Once the program is installed, you can use the same setup routine to uninstall the Control Pad and its components if you want.

The Setup program provides C:\Program Files\ActiveX Control Pad as the default folder to install ActiveX Control Pad. If you do not want to install the program to this location, switch to another folder. Once you have chosen the appropriate install directory, click the Complete button to continue the installation as shown in Figure 1.4.

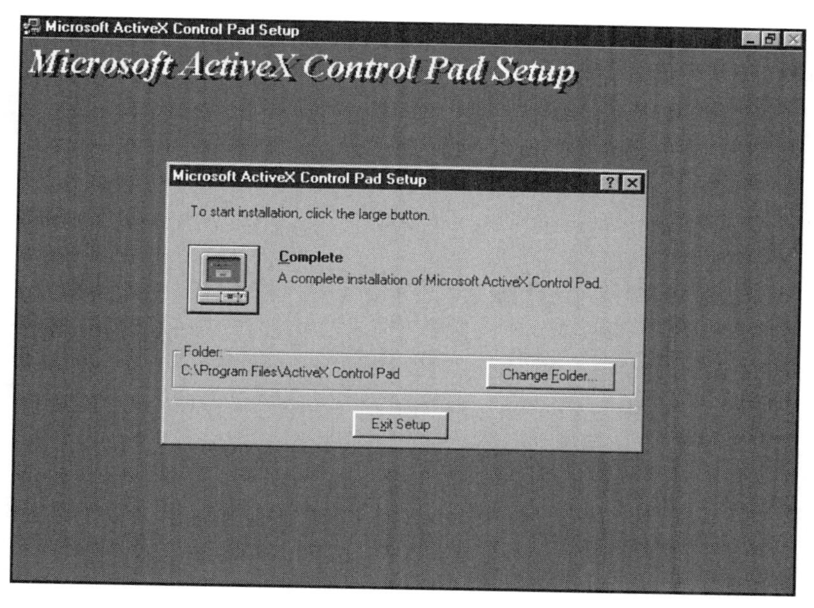

FIGURE 1.4 After choosing the install folder, the installation process will begin copying files to your hard drive.

The last step to the installation is choosing a Program Group for the ActiveX Control program icon to be copied to. This is the icon that you use to access the program itself, so choose a location that's easy for you to remember. The default location is a new folder called Microsoft ActiveX Control Pad. If you do not want the icon placed here, simply choose a new folder and click OK.

Once the program installs, a dialog box appears to inform you that the process was successful. Click OK to exit the installation process. Figure 1.5 illustrates the default Program Group where an icon is created to open the Control Pad.

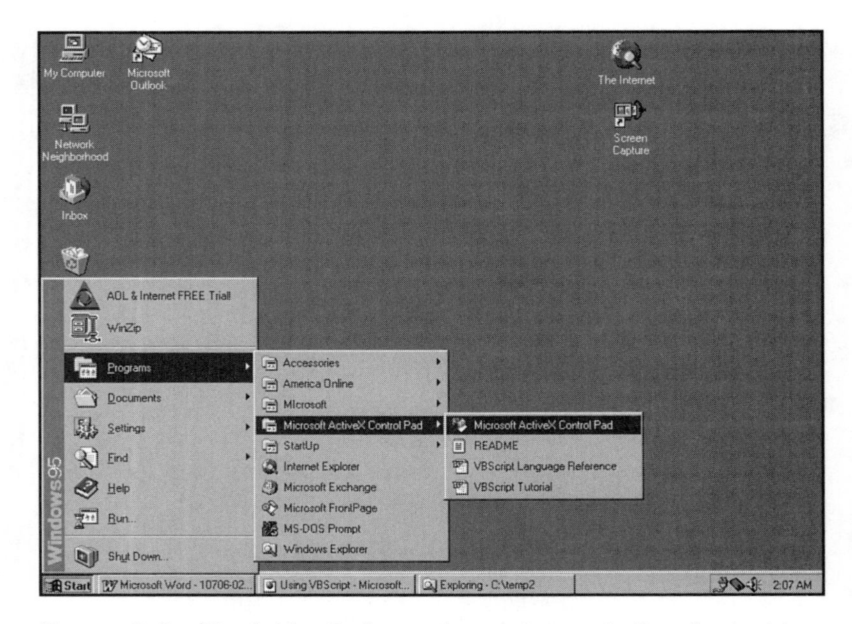

FIGURE 1.5 The folder that you choose to create the shortcut to the program file in is available immediately after the installation routine.

In this lesson, you learned how to download and install the ActiveX Control Pad. In the next lesson, you learn more about the ActiveX Control Pad interface, toolbar, and menu structure.

LESSON 2

Getting Started with ActiveX Control Pad

In this lesson, you will learn how to navigate within the Control Pad's workspace and use menus and toolbars to make your work more productive. Accessing the built-in help system will also be introduced.

Starting the ActiveX Control Pad

If you have installed the Control Pad correctly, you will be able to locate the icon to launch the program from the Start menu. By default, the ActiveX Control Pad is installed in the program group ActiveX Control Pad. If you choose an alternative location for the program file, you will have to locate it from the Start menu also.

To open the ActiveX Control Pad from the Start menu, follow these steps:

1. Click the Start button from the Windows taskbar.
2. Move your mouse pointer up to Programs. The programs menu will expand from the Start menu, allowing you to choose the program group where the Control Pad icon is located.
3. Move the mouse pointer to the Microsoft ActiveX Control Pad group. You will see two different icons that you can access, the Control Pad itself, and a README file that contains up-to-date information about the release of the Control Pad that you have installed.
4. Click Microsoft ActiveX Control Pad to launch the program. As the program is loading into memory, the splash screen will be displayed, and finally a blank document

will load in the Control Pad window for you to begin editing. Figure 2.1 illustrates exactly how to open the program.

I don't have a group called Microsoft ActiveX Control Pad! If you cannot locate the icon or program group for the ActiveX Control Pad, chances are that the program did not install correctly. Before reinstalling, open Windows Explorer to the Program Files directory. Look for a folder called ActiveX Control Pad. If it's there, you can find the icon to launch the program and create a shortcut to your desktop. If you cannot locate it, you will have to reinstall. Follow the directions in Lesson 1 to install the Control Pad correctly.

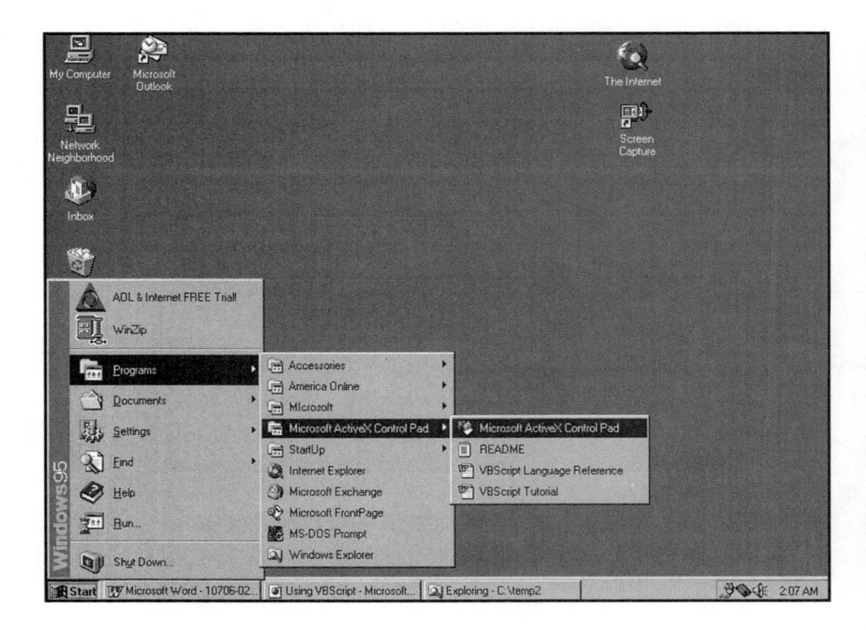

FIGURE 2.1 To launch the Control Pad program file, use the Start menu to find the icon, normally located in the group Microsoft ActiveX Control Pad.

You can also launch the Control Pad by right-clicking an existing HTML document (*.htm, or *.html) from Windows Explorer. Follow these steps to launch the program with an existing file for editing:

1. Click Start, Programs Windows Explorer to launch the program.

2. Locate an existing HTML document on your hard drive or network.

3. Right-click the HTML file and choose Edit with ActiveX Control Pad from the pop-up menu. The Control Pad will launch, with the requested file opened and ready to be edited in the workspace. Figure 2.2 shows the right-click menu in action.

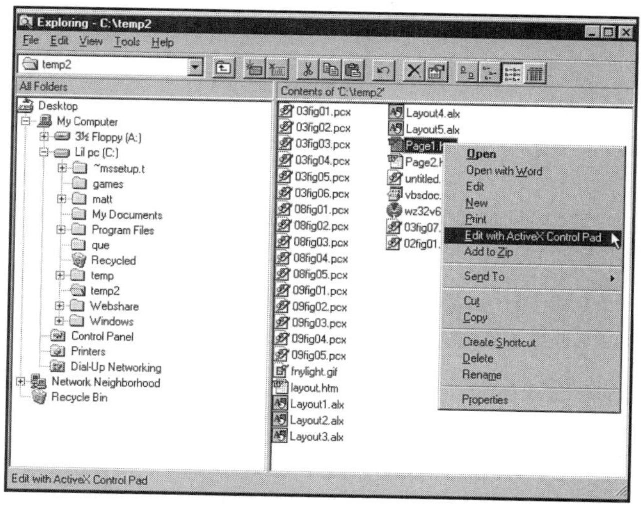

FIGURE 2.2 Using the right-click menu to open existing HTML documents will allow the Control Pad to open with your document in place, allowing you to edit it right away.

When the Control Pad is launched from the Start menu, a blank document titled page1.htm will always open. If you use the right-click method to open a document, only the document that you requested will open within the program.

A Tour of the Control Pad's Workspace

The layout of the Control Pad's workspace will be very familiar to you if you often work with other Microsoft products. At the top of the window you will notice the standard Windows menus from which all of the file, editing, and help functions are accessed. The Control Pad toolbar is located just below the file menu and allows you to access the program functions without clicking through menus or having to remember complex Windows shortcuts. The physical layout of the Control Pad is depicted in Figure 2.3.

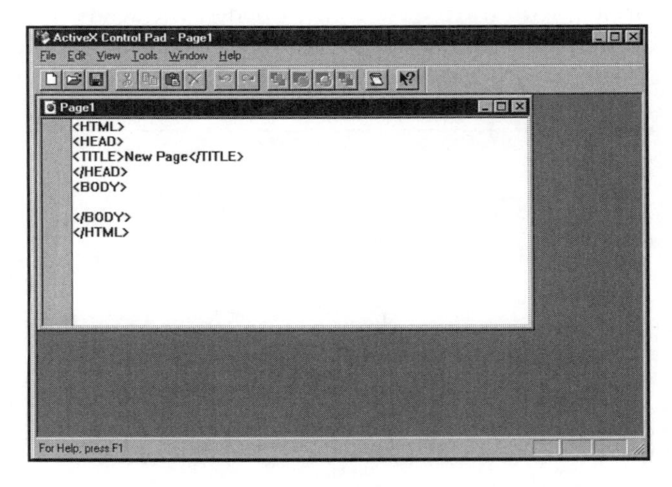

FIGURE 2.3 The Control Pad's workspace looks quite like other Windows-based editing programs through the use of the standard menus and a toolbar for program shortcuts.

Using the Control Pad's Menus

The ActiveX Control Pad contains six pull-down menus located at the top of the program window, just below the title bar. These menus allow you to access all of the functions of the Control Pad through a series of clicks of the mouse on the appropriate function. Each menu contains program functions that relate directly to the menu title. For example, if you wish to create a new file, you would use the File menu to create a new file. If you wish to copy a portion of your document to the Windows' clipboard for later use, you would use the copy function under the Edit menu.

Using the File Menu

The **File** menu controls all of the file functions in the Control Pad program relating to creating, saving, and opening HTML files. The following is a breakdown of the File menu functions:

New HTML Allows the program to create a blank HTML document within the Control Pad ready for editing.

New HTML Layout Creates a blank HTML Layout page for creating a document that will allow you to do exact placement of HTML layout items in your Web pages.

Open Opens an existing HTML or HTML layout document for editing in the Control Pad. A standard Windows dialog box will open allowing you to navigate your file system for a specific document.

Close Closes the file currently open within the Control Pad. If the document has been modified and the changes not saved, you will be prompted to save your changes before the file is closed.

Save Saves the document currently active in the Control Pad window to its location on your hard drive.

Save As Saves the current active file to the location and name of your choice on your hard drive or network.

Save All Saves all open documents at once.

Print Prints the active HTML document to your printer. You will be able to select which printer to send the file to before it is actually printed.

Recent Files A listing of the last four files edited with the Control Pad. To access any of these files quickly, click File and choose the document of your choice.

Exit Closes down every open document within the Control Pad and closes the program.

Nothing is listed in Recent Files! Your list of Recent Files will be blank until you begin creating Web pages and HTML Layout pages with the Control Pad. As you add new pages, they will appear in the Recent Files list in the order that you last used them.

USING THE EDIT MENU

The **Edit** Menu contains 10 items that allow you to edit various parts of your HTML documents and layout pages with a couple of clicks of the mouse. These ten features are:

Undo Removes the last change that you have made from your document.

Redo Adds the last change that you last removed from your document. This function only works when you have just used the Undo command.

Cut Removes a selection of highlighted text from your document and places it on the Windows clipboard for later use.

Copy Copies a selection of highlighted text from your document and places it on the Windows clipboard for later use.

Paste Pastes the contents of the Windows clipboard into your document in the Control Pad.

Delete Deletes all traces of selected text within the active document.

Select All Highlights all text within the active document in the Control Pad.

Insert ActiveX Control Opens a list of all of the registered ActiveX Controls on your system allowing you to choose one to insert into your document.

Insert HTML Layout Inserts a previously created HTML Layout page into your active HTML document.

Edit Object Allows you to edit the properties of a selected ActiveX object from your active HTML document.

Using the View Menu

The View menu controls what components are displayed in your Control Pad workspace. If you wish to remove the selected item, simply click next to the menu item. Only menu items with a check mark on the left side will be displayed. The two options are:

Toolbar Allows the display of the Control Pad Toolbar within the program.

Status Bar Allows messages relating to different Control Pad procedures to be displayed within the bottom of the workspace screen.

Using the Tools Menu

The Tools menu allows you to access the Script Wizard and to set program options within the Control Pad. The two options are:

Script Wizard Launches the Script Wizard which displays all of the events, actions, and other functions of the scripting language used in your document. The default scripting language is VBScript, though you can set your preferences within Options. Be warned however, you can only use one scripting language per HTML page.

Options Enables you to change how the program works through two controls, the Script and HTML Layout properties. Within the Script properties, you can change which Script is the default language (VBScript or JavaScript) and how your actual code will be viewed. The HTML Layout properties allow you to change spacing and adjust grid settings.

USING THE WINDOWS MENU

The **Windows** menu allows you to control how multiple documents appear within the Control Pad and lets you switch between open documents quickly. The three functions of the Windows Menu are:

Cascade Displays all of your open documents on-screen at the same time. The documents will be displayed diagonally down your workspace, allowing you to work on each one with only a mouse click.

Tile Spreads out all of your open documents into a tiled pattern, one next to another.

Pages Allows you to switch between open documents by clicking the document name that you wish to edit.

USING THE HELP MENU

The **Help** menu allows you to find help relating to the Control Pad commands, HTML reference, and scripting reference between VBScript and JavaScript. All of the functions of the Help Menu will be explained within Lesson 3, "Getting Help."

Accessing Help Quickly You can launch the ActiveX Control Pad Help file quickly by pressing F1. Pressing this button will have the same effect as clicking the Help menu and choosing the help topic.

USING THE TOOLBAR

The Control Pad toolbar contains shortcuts to menu-related items, making them accessible with a single mouse click. Figure 2.4 illustrates the conveniently placed toolbar.

Figure 2.4 The Control Pad toolbar allows one-click menu functions while editing your document.

The first nine buttons contained within the Toolbar are shortcuts to the File and Edit menus and should be very familiar to you if you have worked with a word processor. These functions are **New**, **Open**, **Save**, **Cut**, **Copy**, **Paste**, **Delete**, **Undo** and **Redo**. The next six buttons relate directly to HTML Layout, Scripting and the Help system. Table 2.1 contains a brief synopsis of the function of the remaining six toolbar buttons.

TABLE 2.1 THE CONTROL PAD TOOLBAR

BUTTON NAME	FUNCTION
Bring to Front	Moves the selected object to the front of the layout
Move Forward	Moves the selected object forward one layer in the overall layout
Move Backward	Moves the selected object backward one layer in the overall layout
Send to Back	Moves the selected object to the back of the layout
Script Wizard	Opens the Script Wizard with the default scripting language in place
Help	Opens the context-sensitive Help window

OTHER ITEMS IN THE CONTROL PAD'S WORKSPACE

The Control Pad has a few special menus that you will encounter from time to time. When you begin working with the HTML

Layout editor, you will become familiar with the layout designer. If you are familiar with the forms designer in Visual Basic, you will feel right at home working with HTML Layouts and the layout designer.

What is Visual Basic? Visual Basic is a programming language used to author various types of Windows programs. The program itself is appealing because it allows a non-programmer a graceful introduction to the world of programming. Visual Basic is not limited only to simple programs, however. Many of the shareware programs that you can download from the Internet are authored in Visual Basic.

Figure 2.5 shows the layout designer as it will appear inside of the Control Pad.

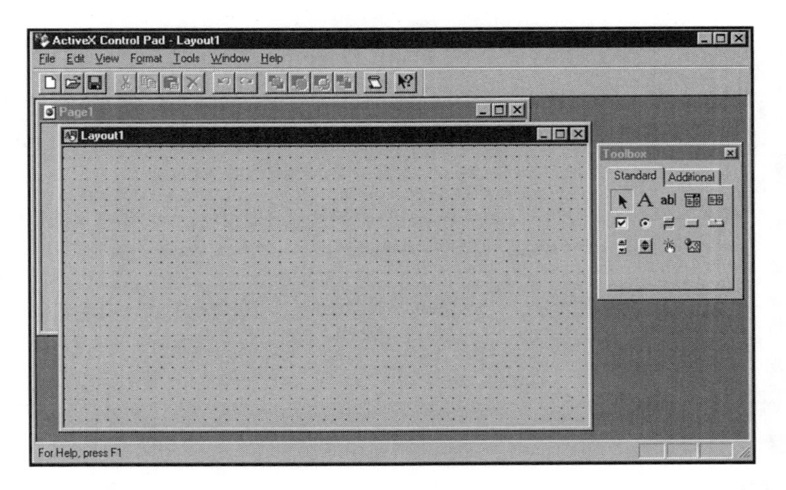

FIGURE 2.5 The layout designer allows you to create form-based controls quite like Visual Basic.

While working with HTML Layouts, you will also become familiar with the ActiveX Toolbox. The toolbox contains a number of ActiveX controls that are accessed by clicking the selected icon. Each ActiveX control will also have a properties window associated with the control's properties, allowing you to modify the function and look of the control itself. The default ActiveX Toolbox is depicted in Figure 2.6.

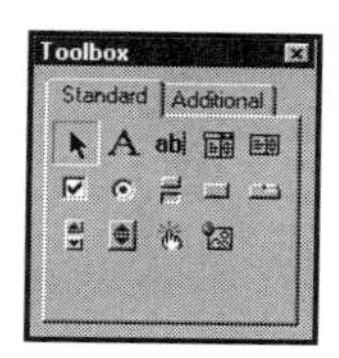

FIGURE 2.6 The ActiveX Toolbox makes it possible to include ActiveX controls within your HTML Layout documents.

The HTML Layout functions are described fully in Lessons 6 through 8.

In this lesson, you became familiar with the Control Pad's interface and toolbar features. In the next lesson, you will learn how to effectively use the ActiveX Control Pad's vast online help system.

LESSON

3 Getting Help

As a result of the ActiveX Control Pad and ActiveX technologies being so new themselves, you will most likely need to access the Control Pad's vast Help system at one time or another. In this lesson, you learn how to access the ActiveX Control Pad's Help system and where to gain additional help on the Internet.

Using the Contents List

Even if you are the most seasoned Visual Basic programming expert, there are times when you need to access the Help system. The Help system contains valuable information about HTML, the different functions of the Control Pad, the Developer's reference, and scripting commands.

To begin using the built-in Help system, use either of the following two methods:

1. Click the Help menu and select Control Pad Help Topics.
2. Press F1 to open the Control Pad Help Topics window.

The ActiveX Control Pad Help system is broken down into five sections called books. These books are comprised of ActiveX Control Pad Basics, Working with Pages, Working with Controls, Scripting, and a Developers reference. The books used to access specific help topics are illustrated in Figure 3.1.

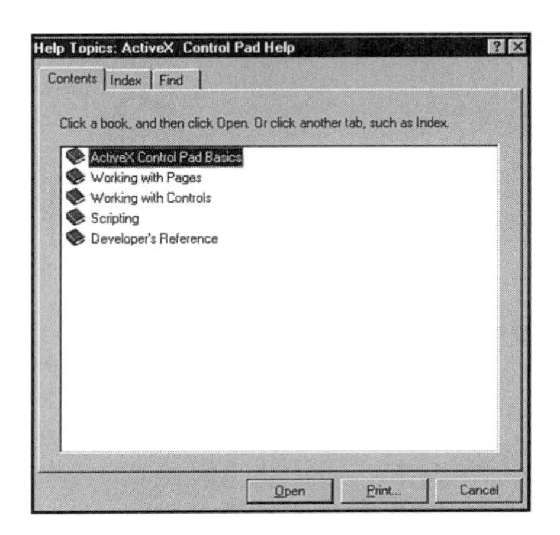

FIGURE 3.1 The Help system defines functions of the Control Pad in detail and also contains valuable scripting and ActiveX control references.

Each of the online books are completely separate references, and can be expanded by a simple double-click. For a great example of this function, follow these steps:

1. Start the Help system by pressing F1.
2. Double-click ActiveX Control Pad Basics to reveal the four sub-topics.

To access any of the sub-topics, you simply double-click the topic name and a dialog box appears with the information that you have selected in the window. If there are sub-topics for the subject that you have chosen, you see another book icon to the left of the topic. Double-clicking this icon expands the tree even more (see Figure 3.2).

To see an example of this, follow these steps:

1. Double-click the Working with Controls subject. The tree expands, displaying a variety of books related to the subject.

2. Double-click Using the ActiveX Control Pad Toolbox. More topics appear. Notice that this sub-topic does not contain any further reference books.

3. Double-click What Is the Toolbox?. The Help subject opens into its own window, allowing you to read the information and print it out if you wish.

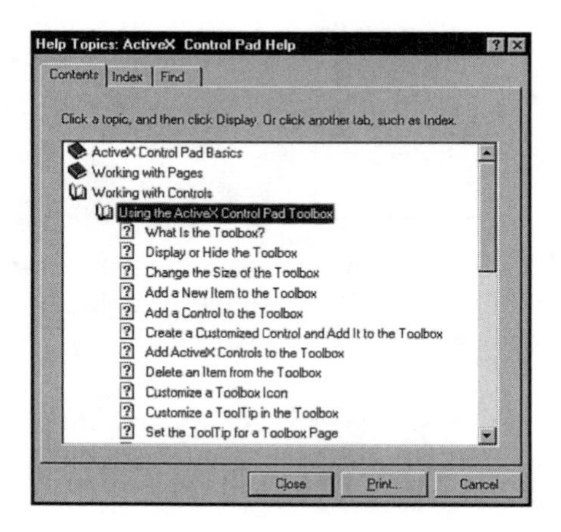

FIGURE 3.2 The Help tree grows as you double-click further into more specific topics.

Once a specific Help topic has been opened, notice that some of the keywords are underlined like hyperlinks on a Web page. To gain further information on a topic simply click its keyword.

Keyword A keyword is a single word or a phrase underlined in blue in a help file. Clicking the keyword will produce one of two possible results. Either a pop-up window will appear with a definition of the keyword, or a new help page will open and explain the topic in depth.

USING THE INDEX

There are times when the topics contained within the top level of the Help system do not offer you the help that you need. If you have a specific keyword that you are looking for, you may find it easier to use the Index feature rather than browsing through the entire Help system.

To open the Index feature of the Help system, follow these steps:

1. Press F1 to start the Help system.
2. Click the Index tab. A text box appears followed by an entire range of alphabetically indexed keywords.

After opening the Index portion of the Help system, it is now time to type the word or keywords into the text box at the top of the Help Topics dialog box. One of the most powerful features of the Index system is that your results appear on-the-fly. As you type your keywords into the Index system, the Help system immediately locates and displays topics. Follow these steps to search the Index for information:

1. With the Index feature open, type **code view** into the text box. Notice that the moment you begin typing into the box, the Help system begins trying to find the information you are looking for. Each keystroke that you type will cause the help file to search its index list alphabetically until it locates the term you are looking for.
2. Double-click the Choosing sub-topic in the list. A context-sensitive help window appears, showing information about the subject that you have chosen. Figure 3.3 shows the results of the term that you are searching for.

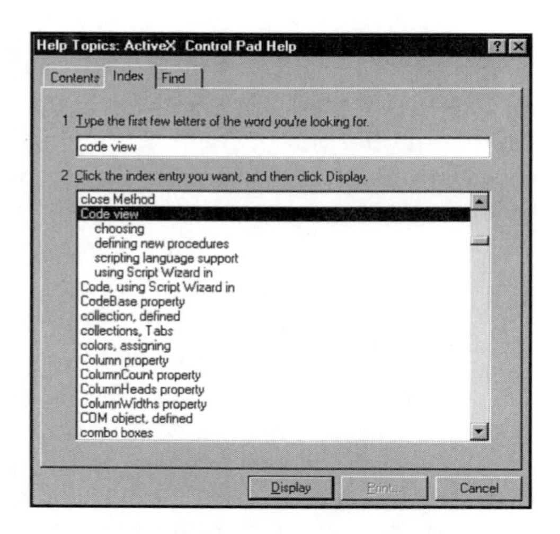

FIGURE 3.3 The term or terms that you search for under the Index feature are available as soon as you type the first few letters of the words you are looking for.

As you can see, it is very easy to do a keyword or phrase search with the Index feature of the Help system. Using this feature can save you valuable time when searching for information, and is much more efficient than delving down into the Help topics themselves.

ACCESSING THE HTML REFERENCE

There are so many HTML tags that exist today that even the most seasoned HTML veteran needs help at one time or another. The ActiveX Control Pad is installed with a helpful resource for all of Internet Explorer 3.0 HTML tags. This feature, though accessed through the Help system, appears through Internet Explorer itself. This is one of the reasons that Internet Explorer 3.0 had to be installed before installing the ActiveX Control Pad.

To gain access to the HTML reference, click Help, HTML Reference. After a few seconds, Internet Explorer appears and displays the HTML Reference section. One really nice feature of accessing the HTML Reference through Internet Explorer is that you can cut and paste the HTML tags directly into your documents. The HTML reference file is illustrated in Figure 3.4.

Bookmark the HTML Reference Page To provide quick access to the HTML reference page in the future, click Favorites, Add to Favorites to create a handy bookmark. When you want to use the HTML reference page in the future, simply click Favorites from the menu in Internet Explorer and choose the HTML Reference bookmark.

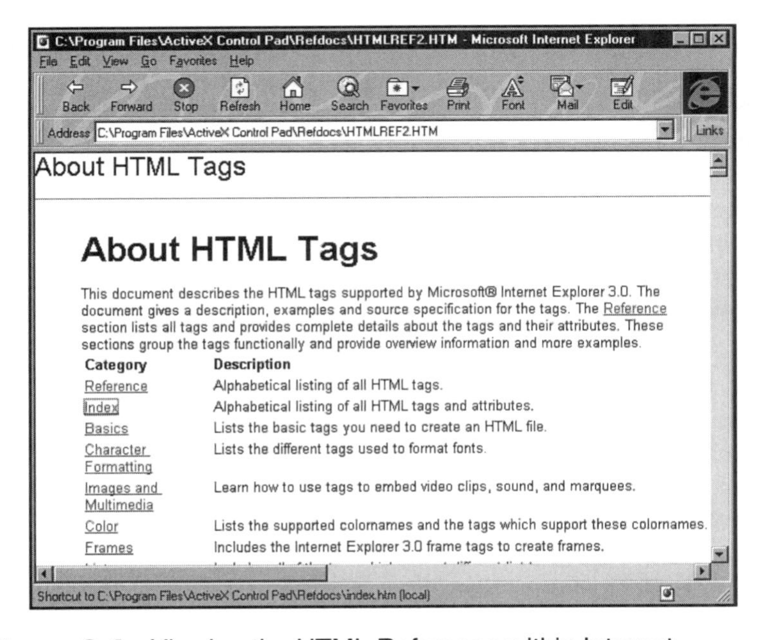

FIGURE 3.4 Viewing the HTML Reference within Internet Explorer is a quick way to navigate and save HTML tag specifications.

The HTML reference is very extensive because it not only shows the HTML tags but also defines those tags and allows you to choose the one that is right for you. For example, if you are looking for information on including a marquee into your document, find the most in-depth information by following these steps:

1. With the HTML reference open in Internet Explorer, click Index in the HTML Reference Web page. The Index page will open, displaying a long list of indexed HTML elements.
2. Click M from the alphabet listing. The Index page will instantly jump down to the section that begins with M.
3. Choose Marquee from the listing. All of the relevant HTML attributes relating to the `<MARQUEE>` tag appear.

ACCESSING THE VBSCRIPT REFERENCE

Before you can access the VBScript Reference you must download and install the additional Help file. Microsoft most likely did this to reduce the size of the ActiveX Control Pad for downloading. To download the VBScript help file, point your Web browser to **http://www.microsoft.com/vbscript/us/download/vbsdown.htm**.

Once you download and install the help file, you are instantly able to access the VBScript Reference from the Help menu. The VBScript Reference, like the HTML Reference, appears in your default Web browser so you can bookmark pages to which you most often refer. Figure 3.5 demonstrates the VBScript help file accessed in Internet Explorer.

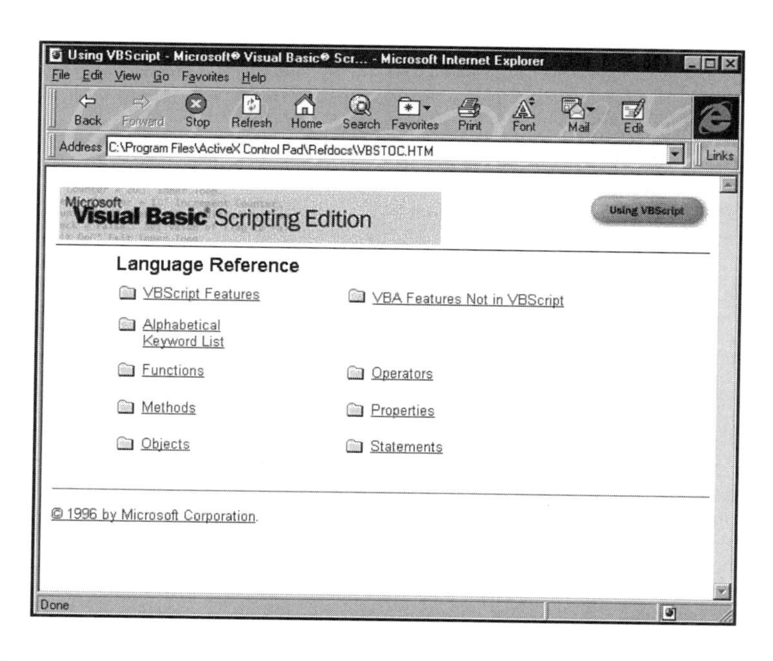

FIGURE 3.5 The VBScript help file is displayed within your default web browser, just like the HTML Reference.

GETTING HELP ON THE INTERNET

Even though Microsoft has included a vast amount of support information within the Help system, sometimes you need more help than the Help system can provide. There are a variety of ways to access more help from the Internet itself.

Some of the most valuable resources for gaining additional information about the ActiveX Control Pad are the free newsgroups at **news.microsoft.com**. Once you subscribe to these newsgroups, you have access to over 200 public newsgroups covering a number of topics. One newsgroup that you want to specifically checkout is **microsoft.public.activex.controlpad**. This newsgroup is dedicated to the ActiveX Control Pad and allows individuals to post questions and search for answers on any questions that they might have.

Newsgroups Newsgroups are a collection of bulletin boards where Internet users can post messages about a specific topic and read other postings. There are over 15,000 different newsgroups currently available on USENET newsgroups ranging from fine arts to specific computer programs. Ask your Internet Service Provider or Network Administrator how you can access USENET newsgroups through your Internet connection.

Another valuable resource for finding out about ActiveX technologies is the Site Builder Workshop located at **http://www.microsoft.com/sitebuilder/**. Microsoft created this site as a resource that covers every Internet technology that the company is currently working on. The site itself is broken down into categories such as Authoring/Editing, Design/Creative, Programming, Planning/Production, and Site Administration. The site is updated often and provides a wealth of information regarding site building and incorporating new technologies such as ActiveX Controls.

In 1996, the ActiveX Control Specification was handed over to this independent body to insure that ActiveX is developed fairly and used to its full potential. You can track the status of the ActiveX standards at **http://www.activex.org/**. This Web site is produced by a group made up of many companies, including Microsoft, and provides a wealth of resources and news as they relate to ActiveX controls and development.

In this lesson, you learned the various ways of accessing ActiveX Control Pad's Help system, the HTML Reference, and the VBScript Reference. You also learned a few ways of becoming more familiar with the Control Pad through resources found on the Internet. In the next lesson, you learn how to use the Object Editor to incorporate ActiveX controls into HTML documents.

LESSON 4

Adding ActiveX Controls to Your Web Page

In this lesson, you learn how to use the ActiveX Control Pad to create a Web page and then insert an ActiveX control into your document.

Creating a Web Page

There are many programs available at retail stores or downloadable from the Internet today that make creating Web pages as easy as typing and formatting a letter in Microsoft Word. The HTML editor that is bundled with the ActiveX Control Pad enables you to create robust HTML applications, although you have to know some HTML tags before your page turns out the way that you want it to look.

Many Web authors are using Control Pad to insert ActiveX controls into their documents, and are then copying and pasting the HTML code in another editor. While Control Pad is great for automatically adding ActiveX controls to a Web page, it is not as advanced as many other HTML editors.

Microsoft has recently included the functionality of the ActiveX Control Pad in Front Page 97, a visual HTML authoring program. The Control Pad and Script Wizard are implemented fully in this release, though you will access them from a different set of menus than you are usually accustomed to seeing. By including the features of the ActiveX Control Pad into this new authoring tool, Microsoft has completed a powerful Web development tool that has the functionality of many HTML programs. One of the greatest features of Front Page 97 is the fact that all of your HTML is entered into the program, much like you would if you were working with a word processor. You actually don't need to know any HTML to become productive with Front Page 97.

Word Processor A word processor is used for authoring text documents such as letters, reports, and brochures. Many word processors, such as Microsoft Word, come with the ability to open and edit HTML documents easily, though you can author HTML in virtually every word processor. A tool like this can be especially helpful when authoring large documents that require advanced editing functions such as Find, and Search and Replace.

When you open ActiveX Control Pad, an HTML page appears, virtually empty except for the required tags. If you need to create a new HTML page in Control Pad, use either of the following two methods:

- Choose File, New HTML. An HTML template appears.
- You can also click the New HTML button on the toolbar to create a new page in Control Pad or press Ctrl+N to achieve the same results.

When the HTML page appears, it, as yet, contains no formatting; you have to add the content. If you saved the HTML document right now and viewed it in your Web browser, you would simply see an empty page.

What do all of these codes mean? The HTML document template that appears when you create a new HTML page in the Control Pad contains a number of HTML tags that should appear in your HTML page for it to function properly. These tags are defined in Table 4.1.

TABLE 4.1 HTML TAGS NEEDED FOR A PROPER FUNCTIONING HTML PAGE

HTML TAG NAME	DESCRIPTION
`<HTML>`	Denotes the beginning of an HTML file.
`<HEAD>`	Marks the place in the HTML document where the heading information like the title will appear.
`<TITLE>`	The title of your HTML document that will appear at the top of the user's browser when the page is loaded.
`<BODY>`	The beginning of the document content. All of the document content will be entered between the `<BODY>` `</BODY>` tags.

Each HTML tag has a matching tag that begins with a forward slash. This symbol represents closure for the tag, and allows the next HTML section to begin. Though it's not always necessary, it is correct HTML authoring practice to close every HTML tag statement with an identical tag that begins with the / character.

Follow these steps to add a title to your new document:

1. Select `New Page` between the `<TITLE></TITLE>` tags.
2. Type the words **My First ActiveX Control Page**.

   The next step is to add a little text within the body of your HTML document.

3. Place your mouse cursor between the `<BODY>` and `</BODY>` tags.
4. Type the following HTML code:
   <H1>ActiveX Controls are easy to use</H1>

   This creates a large heading at the top of your HTML document.

5. Choose File, Save to save your changes. You can rename the file to something a bit easier to remember than Page1.htm if you want. Just remember where you saved the file.

Saving HTML Files You can save an HTML file with an extension of .htm or .html. The .htm extension was originally used on Windows 3.1 computers that could not handle file extensions with more than three characters. In Windows 95 and Windows NT use whichever file extension you prefer. Note that the .html extension is the most widely used on the Internet.

6. Start Internet Explorer and choose File, Open, Browse and locate the file that you just created. Click the Open button to view your page. Figure 4.1 illustrates what your new page will look like within the browser.

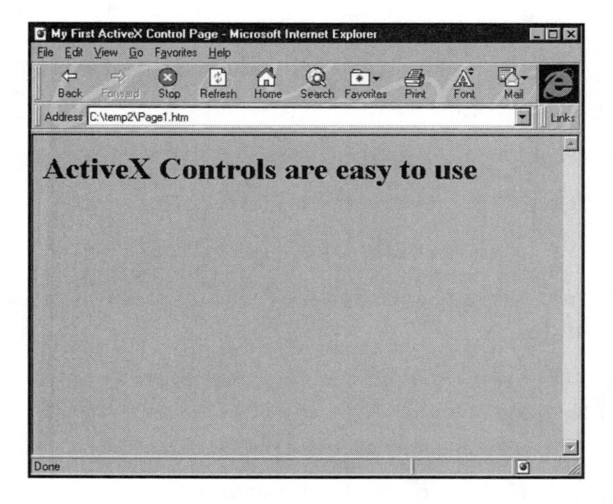

FIGURE 4. 1 Learning the basics of HTML is rather easy, but mastering all of HTML can take years.

SELECTING AND INSERTING AN ACTIVEX CONTROL

You have the basics of your first Web page laid out, and now you are ready to add your first ActiveX control. The control that you are going insert in your Web page is called the Label Control, which is one of the simplest ActiveX controls to use. This control displays a piece of formatted text within your Web page. It can take on different appearances by using different font names, font sizes, colors, and much more.

Inserting an ActiveX control is as simple as choosing that control from a menu. Follow these steps to insert your ActiveX control:

1. Choose Edit, Insert ActiveX Control. The Insert ActiveX Control dialog box appears, allowing you to choose the control that you want to insert.
2. Click Microsoft IE30 Label Control and click OK.

I don't have a control called Microsoft IE30 Label! Not all of the controls that are used in this book come with Internet Explorer or the Control Pad. You may need to download further components from Microsoft's Web site. Refer to Lesson 18 for the instructions you need to download additional controls. Once you have downloaded the control, close and restart the Control Pad. The control that you need will be available from the menu.

Once you click OK, the Object Editor window appears. The Object Editor is responsible for visually editing all of the different aspects of an ActiveX control. The Object Editor is illustrated in Figure 4.2.

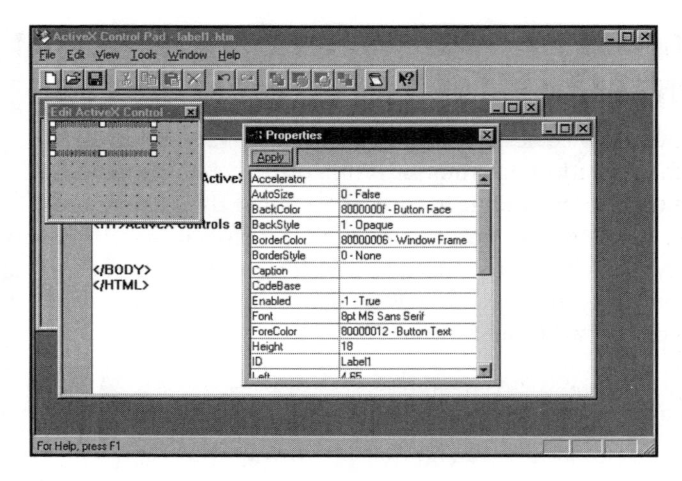

FIGURE 4.2 The Object Editor appears as soon as you insert a new ActiveX control into your HTML document.

What is the Edit ActiveX Control window? You'll notice that two windows actually open when you insert or edit an ActiveX control. The Edit ActiveX Control window appears with the Object Editor and allows you to see a visible copy of the ActiveX control you just inserted. Within this window, you can resize the image with your mouse and see exactly what the control will look like when it's inserted into your Web page (see Figure 4.2).

All of a control's available properties are listed within the Object Editor and can be modified through a series of mouse clicks and new entries into the property box. The Object Editor automatically opens when you add an ActiveX control to your Web page. This is so you can change a control's properties before it is inserted into the page. For now, close the Object Editor by clicking the X in the upper-right corner.

After you close the Object Editor, the Label Control is automatically inserted into your HTML document. You know that you have inserted it correctly when you see new HTML code that appears between the `<OBJECT></OBJECT>` tags.

MODIFYING CONTROLS WITH THE OBJECT EDITOR

Once you have inserted an ActiveX control into your document, you can change any of its available properties by selecting the property that you want to change in the Object Editor and giving it a new value.

Properties The appearance and function of an ActiveX control is changed through manipulating properties of the control within the Object Editor. Each control has a unique set of properties that control everything, from how it appears on a Web page to whether or not it is visible when the Web page is loaded. Some controls have many properties, while some may only have a handful. Becoming familiar with property functions is made easier by the fact that many controls share the same properties.

Before the release of ActiveX Control Pad, all ActiveX controls built into Web pages had to be authored by hand. This involved a set of tedious steps that required the author to be familiar with all of a control's properties and knowing how to find out a control's `CLASSID` value. Now, it's all just a few mouse clicks from beginning to end.

You can begin editing the properties of your control by opening the Object Editor inside Control Pad. To do so, use the following steps:

1. Click the button of Control Pad that is located just to the left of the `<OBJECT>` tags. As you pass your mouse over it, the button's name appears, Edit ActiveX Control. The Edit ActiveX Control icon is depicted in Figure 4.3.

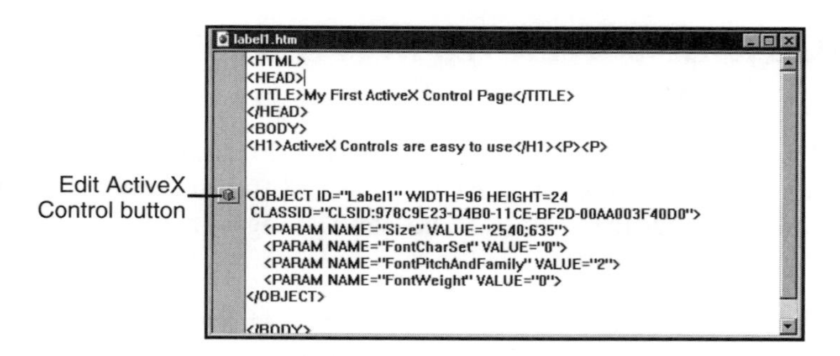
label1.htm
<HTML>
<HEAD>
<TITLE>My First ActiveX Control Page</TITLE>
</HEAD>
<BODY>
<H1>ActiveX Controls are easy to use</H1><P><P>
<OBJECT ID="Label1" WIDTH=96 HEIGHT=24
CLASSID="CLSID:978C9E23-D4B0-11CE-BF2D-00AA003F40D0">
<PARAM NAME="Size" VALUE="2540;635">
<PARAM NAME="FontCharSet" VALUE="0">
<PARAM NAME="FontPitchAndFamily" VALUE="2">
<PARAM NAME="FontWeight" VALUE="0">
</OBJECT>
Edit ActiveX Control button

FIGURE 4. 3 The Edit ActiveX Control button is a quick way to start the Object Editor in Control Pad.

2. Drag the title bar of the Object Editor to an area that allows you to view your HTML code. By doing this, you can observe the changes being made to the HTML as you edit the control.

At this point, your new control is not much to look at. It has no caption and no color. There's actually nothing that distinguishes the control from the rest of your HTML page.

The first change that you make to the Label Control is to change the color of the background so it stands apart from the rest of the Web page. To achieve this, you modify the `BackColor` property.

BackColor The BackColor property controls the background color of a property or component being displayed. You will only see a change in the back color of a control if the BackStyle property is set to Opaque. This will allow your control to have a solid background instead of appearing transparent.

Use the following steps the make your Label Control stand out:

1. Click within the `BackColor` property value in the Object Editor. The `BackColor` line is now highlighted and the current value of `BackColor` appears at the top of the Object Editor window.

2. Click the ellipsis button in the upper-right corner of the Object Editor window. You can select a new color for the background color of the Label Control.

Ellipses Button The ellipses button is a great feature because it tells you that a new property value can be selected from a list or window instead of by hand. This can be a great timesaver instead of having to remember complicated codes or special property values.

3. Choose a light shade of red and click OK. The new color immediately takes effect in the Edit ActiveX Control menu which appeared when the Object Editor was launched.

4. Click Apply to ensure that your control saves the changes that were last made. Figure 4.4 shows the color change that will occur.

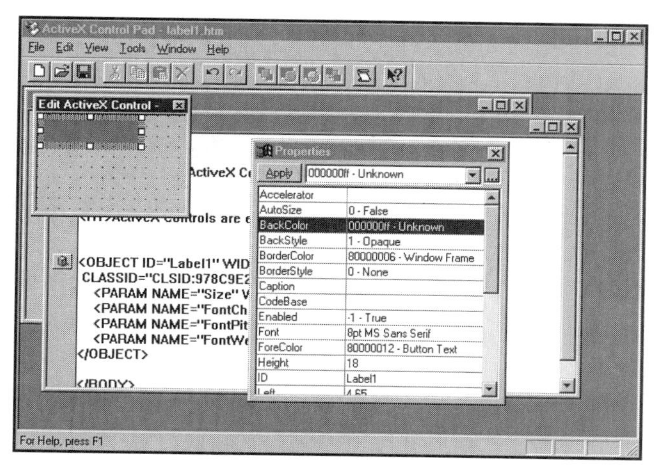

FIGURE 4.4 Physical changes to an ActiveX Control appear in the Edit ActiveX Control window as soon as you change the property.

You have just edited one of the properties of the ActiveX control that you inserted into your HTML document. You could have just as easily changed any other property in the Object Editor by selecting the property name and changing the value at the top. For now, however, this is all of the editing that you need to do.

SAVING AND VIEWING YOUR WEB PAGE

Now that you have added an ActiveX Control and changed one of the properties, it's time that you viewed your work. Follow these steps to save your work and view your page in Internet Explorer:

1. Click File, Save As. The Save As dialog box will appear.
2. Create a new folder on your hard drive called Temp if you do not already have one. You can do this by clicking the Create New Folder button in the dialog box.
3. Save the file as Label1.htm in the File Name text box. Click OK to save.
4. Start Internet Explorer and choose File, Open. When the Open dialog box appears, click Browse. Move to the Temp folder and double-click the Label1.htm file.

The HTML file that contains your first ActiveX control appears, displaying the red label whose property you just changed. The Web page containing the Label control will look like Figure 4.5.

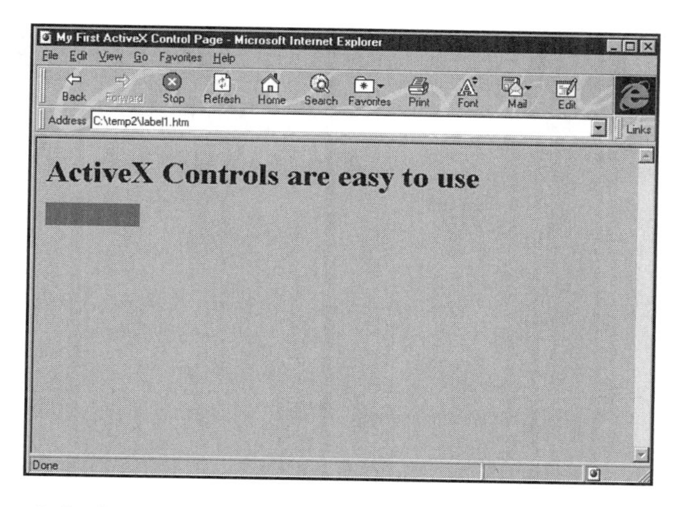

FIGURE 4.5 You have taken a big step in learning about ActiveX controls, and yet there are still many more properties that you can change.

In this lesson, you learned how to create a new HTML file, insert an ActiveX control, and modify properties using the Object Editor. In the next lesson, you learn different ways of modifying an ActiveX control's properties and experiment by changing additional property values.

LESSON 5

Customizing ActiveX Controls

In this lesson, you learn how to edit the properties of an ActiveX Control both visually and manually.

Editing Control Properties

Before you begin editing the properties of an ActiveX control, you need to make sure that you fully understand how to insert a control into your page. You can practice by creating a page with a window to type comments into using the Microsoft Text Box control, then creating a series of buttons that would normally be used to send the form and reset its contents. Don't be concerned with making the page look pretty, just experiment by adding multiple controls. For assistance in creating this sample control page, refer to Lesson 4, "Adding ActiveX Controls to Your Web Page."

Now it's time to adjust the properties of a control to change the way it appears on-screen. Create a new HTML page that contains a Label control. Make sure that the Label is big enough in size so that you leave plenty of space to work with. Save the file as Label1.htm.

You can edit an ActiveX control in two very different ways. Before the ActiveX control is inserted into your HTML document, you can use the Property Editor to modify any of its unique properties. Or you can edit the properties of the control manually within the HTML page itself after the control has been inserted into the page.

Editing Controls Manually As long as the changes that you need to make to a control's properties are simple and quick, you will save a lot of time by editing an HTML document by hand instead of with the Control Pad. Many changes, such as those for a caption or the name of a control itself, can be updated much more quickly if you adjust the settings in the HTML file instead of loading it into the Control Pad.

The first method is generally the easiest, though it only works if you have the ActiveX Control Pad installed on the system you are working on. If, however, you are at a remote site and need to adjust the properties of an existing control on a Web page, editing the properties manually is the only solution. Many times it is much simpler to adjust various properties of an inserted control by editing the HTML directly. If you need only change the `Caption` property on a Command Button or the foreground color on a Label Control, usually adjusting these settings manually is much quicker. It is quite hard to remember every property for each control, so do not expect to do all of your editing by hand. The Property Editor makes it very easy to adjust all of a control's properties without guessing what the name of the property is.

EDITING CONTROLS VISUALLY

Using the Property Editor to visually change a control's properties is by far the easiest method to use. All of the property names are displayed within the Property Editor, so you do not have to guess property names when you are changing a control. It is also great because many properties, such as those that change the color of an object, present you with a menu of choices to select from. Otherwise, you could be guessing at color values for hours while your Web page remains down. Even if you download additional controls off of the Internet, once these controls are registered, or installed, on your system, you can begin using them right away with the Control Pad and edit their properties with the Property Editor.

Downloading Controls Some controls that will be introduced in the following lessons will need to be downloaded from Microsoft's Web site on the Internet. The ActiveX Control Gallery, located at **http://www.microsoft.com/activex/gallery/**, houses a collection of controls that have been deemed "safe" by Microsoft. A safe control is one that has been registered and found not to harm your system when activated. Once you download a new control, the registry is updated with the CLASSID of the control and available to the Control Pad.

To begin editing properties of a control with the Property Editor, follow these steps:

1. Start the ActiveX Control Pad.
2. Choose File, Open and locate the file Label1.htm that you saved on your hard drive. The file appears with the HTML containing your inserted Label Control.
3. Click the Edit ActiveX Control button located to the left of the `<OBJECT>` tag. The Property Editor appears with all of the Label Control's properties available for editing. Figure 5.1 illustrates how the Property Editor will look with the Label control loaded.

You are now ready to adjust some of the properties of your inserted Label Control. To begin editing, follow these steps:

1. Click the `Caption` property in the Property Editor. As of now your label has no caption, so the text box at the top is empty.
2. Place your cursor at the top of the Property Editor and type **My Label** in the text box. This eventually shows the words "My Label" on the face of the Label Control.
3. Click the Apply button. This instantly makes your changes permanent. Figure 5.2 illustrates the Apply button in the Property Editor that is used to save changes.

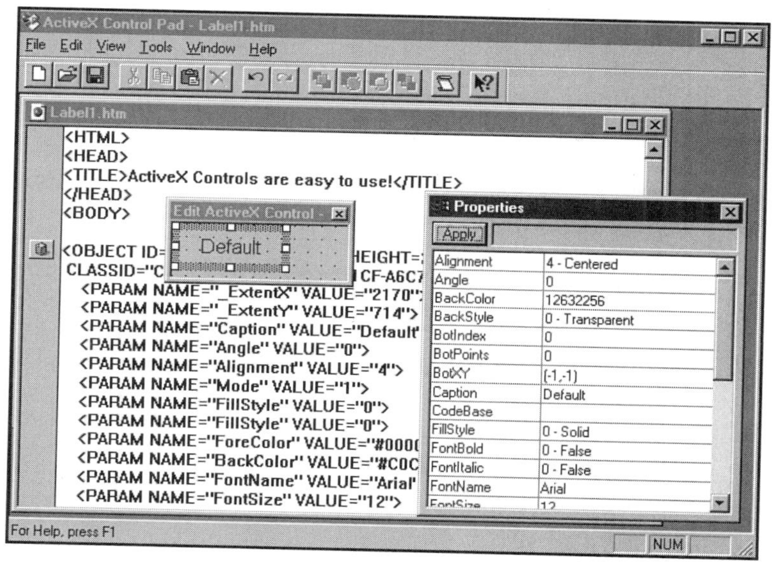

FIGURE 5. 1 The Property Editor appears as soon as you click the Edit ActiveX Control button to the left of your HTML code.

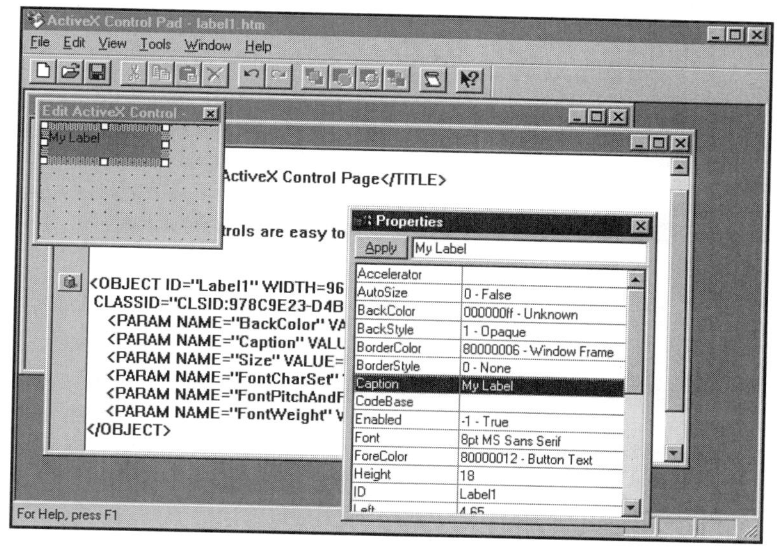

FIGURE 5. 2 The Apply button takes any property changes that you have made and makes them instantly visible.

There are quite a few properties that you can edit easily. You can easily change the color of the Label Control, the font, the font size, the height and width of the control, and the text alignment. You can make all of the changes by clicking in the property that you want to change and typing a new value for the property in the top text box. Make sure that you click the Apply button after every change so that none of your adjustments are lost.

Entering Property Values Quickly Instead of clicking Apply every time you adjust the value of a property, try hitting the Enter key. It has the same effect as the Apply button, but saves you the time of moving the mouse and clicking the button every time you want a change to be permanent.

After you save your HTML file, you can open and view the page in Internet Explorer. Choose File, Open, Browse and locate the file Label1.htm on your hard drive. Once you click Open in the Open dialog box, the file loads and looks much like the Web page seen in Figure 5.3.

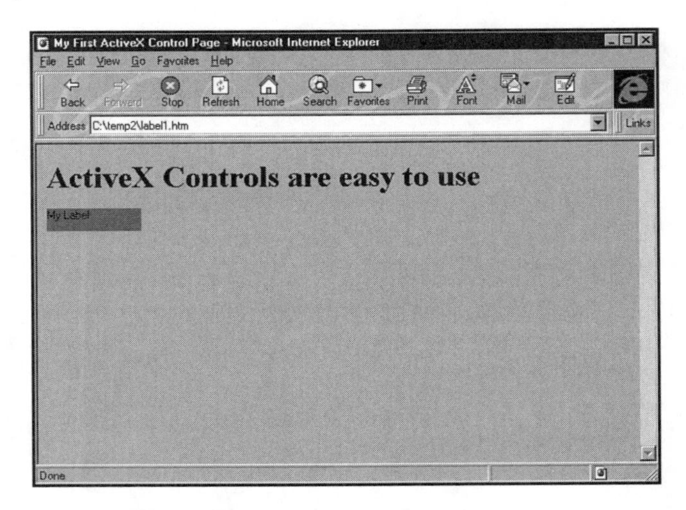

FIGURE 5.3 Because you are only modifying a few properties within your inserted ActiveX Control, the finished Web page should always load with no problems.

EDITING CONTROLS MANUALLY

All of the properties that are available for you to edit visually in the Property Editor are also available by manually typing the property name and value directly into your HTML document. This is especially useful when you do not have access to Control Pad and need to edit an ActiveX control right away.

If you examine a snippet of HTML code from an inserted ActiveX control, you will notice that the control always has a <PARAM> tag that contains a value. This tag should not scare you if you have never seen it before. The <PARAM> tag is simply an additional parameter, or property, that you may want to modify in ActiveX control. Font size, color, and physical dimensions are all parameters that specify how an ActiveX control appears and functions on-screen. Listing 5.1 demonstrates the use of the <PARAM> tag in your HTML page so far:

LISTING 5.1 Properties are listed as parameters in HTML code

```
<OBJECT ID="Label1" WIDTH=96 HEIGHT=24
 CLASSID="CLSID:978C9E23-D4B0-11CE-BF2D-00AA003F40D0">
    <PARAM NAME="Caption" VALUE="My Label">
    <PARAM NAME="Size" VALUE="2540;635">
    <PARAM NAME="FontCharSet" VALUE="0">
    <PARAM NAME="FontPitchAndFamily" VALUE="2">
    <PARAM NAME="FontWeight" VALUE="0">
</OBJECT>
End Listing
```

The `Caption` property that you adjusted earlier in the lesson is reflected in Listing 5.1. You simply changed the original empty value to `"My Label"`.

Now you are going to edit the same property manually. You can change the caption to reflect a new value of `"Changed Label"`. Follow these steps:

1. Within the HTML coding window, highlight the words `My Label`. Do not highlight the quotation marks. These marks

must be in place or else the Label Control cannot display the caption.

2. Type the words **Changed Label**.
3. Click the Save button on the toolbar.
4. Reload the Web page in Internet Explorer to view your changes. Figure 5.4 illustrates the changes that you've made to your Label control.

FIGURE 5.4 Changing the properties of an ActiveX control

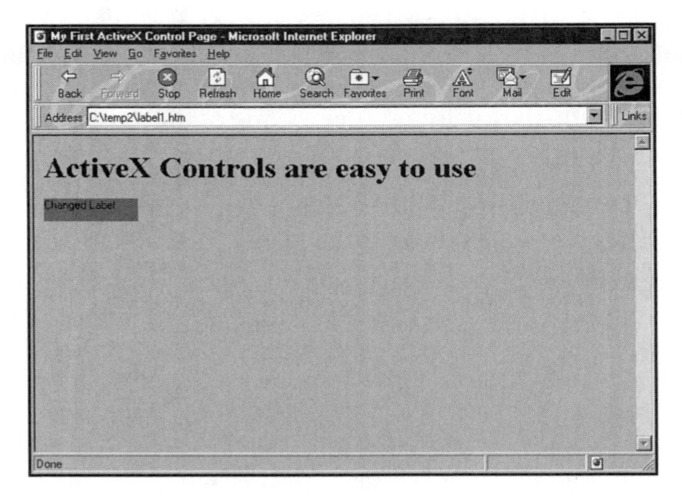

manually makes no difference as to how the control appears.

Since the ActiveX control's properties are stated within the HTML page itself, it does not matter if you change a property value with the Property Editor or by hand.

You might find that this method of editing ActiveX control properties is much quicker than using the Property Editor. While this might be the case, it is very difficult to actually add an ActiveX control by hand. Manual editing is great for changing the properties of existing controls, however.

Feel free to experiment by manually changing any of the properties of the Label Control within the HTML document and reloading the changed page in Internet Explorer.

In this lesson, you learned how to edit the properties of an ActiveX control visually, using the Property Editor, and manually by changing the HTML code directly. In the next lesson, you learn how HTML Layout can effectively make your Web pages display graphics exactly as you want them to appear.

LESSON 6

Understanding HTML Layouts

In this lesson, you become familiar with HTML Layouts and learn how they can help you develop visually pleasing sites.

What Are HTML Layouts?

HTML authors have had to face many limiting factors when designing the graphic layout for Web pages. Through the use of tables and very specific image sizing, Web authors have moved past many of the headaches that are involved with developing a Web page that turns out looking exactly as the author intended. The one problem that remains, however, is that the author can never guarantee how a given page looks because of the numerous different types of browsers that are used to view the content.

HTML Tables Before HTML Layout, the only way to effectively control how graphics on a Web page were displayed was through the use of tables written in HTML. These tables look much like a spreadsheet page in Microsoft Excel. Though the HTML author has total control over how a table is displayed, creating a complex layout with tables can be a nightmare to author, even for the seasoned HTML veteran.

Not all browsers are built alike. Even though there is an HTML specification, many tags are not interpreted the same way. Depending on which browser you are using, and the type of operating system your computer uses, what you see displayed in your Web browser will not necessarily be what your co-worker sees.

America Online's browser, for instance, cannot use scripting languages, Java applets, or Shockwave programs. Lynx, a text-based browser, cannot display anything at all but simple text. Even the same versions of Internet Explorer 3.0 for Windows and Macintosh cannot display the same content. The Macintosh browser is still limited without VBScript and ActiveX controls. Microsoft hopes to remedy this situation with their proposed HTML Layout specification.

HTML Layout is actually implemented as an ActiveX Control, and inserted into a Web page between the `<OBJECT></OBJECT>` tags just like any other control. What happens is that the Layout Control references an outside text file that contains all of the formatting instructions that the browser follows when parsing the HTML file. As soon as the browser downloads the HTML page, your browser parses the associated layout file and displays the contents of the file for the viewer to see.

Parse When a Web browser encounters an HTML page it must parse, or interpret, the instructions contained within. You might think that parsing a Web page is what takes so long for it to open, but the actual process is relatively quick.

Layout File Extensions The default extension for referenced HTML layout files is .Alx. For now, this is the only file that can be referenced and displayed as HTML Layout.

The following is an example of the syntax of an actual layout file:

```
<DIV ID="Layout3"
➥STYLE="LAYOUT:FIXED;WIDTH:477pt;HEIGHT:75pt;">
  <OBJECT ID="Image1"
```

```
    CLASSID="CLSID:D4A97620-8E8F-11CF-93CD-
➥00AA00C08FDF"
STYLE="TOP:8pt;LEFT:8pt;WIDTH:198pt;
➥HEIGHT:66pt;ZINDEX:0;">
     <PARAM NAME="PicturePath"
➥VALUE="c:\temp2\fnylight.gif">
   </OBJECT>
</DIV>
```

Be happy to know that you do not have to know what any of the previous commands are in order to create an HTML layout page. ActiveX Control Pad takes care of creating the actual .Alx file, allowing you to concentrate on designing your Web page exactly the way you want it to look.

WHAT CAN HTML LAYOUTS DO?

Have you ever wanted to place one graphic on top of another or create a Web page that had graphics in a circular pattern rather than a square- or rectangular-based pattern? When using HTML layouts, the sky is the limit when it comes to designing and arranging graphics.

I'm no graphics expert! You don't have to be a graphics expert to use HTML Layout effectively. In fact, you can develop quite a bit of Web content with the ActiveX controls included with the HTML Layout editor.

HTML Layout allows you exact placement, down to one pixel, of any given graphic or ActiveX control. This means that where any given element is placed at design time is exactly where it appears when it is viewed in a Web browser. If you need two buttons in a form to line up perfectly, you can use HTML layout to ensure that these buttons are placed precisely where you want them to appear, without having to worry about complex HTML commands. An example of precise control with HTML Layout is illustrated in Figure 6.1.

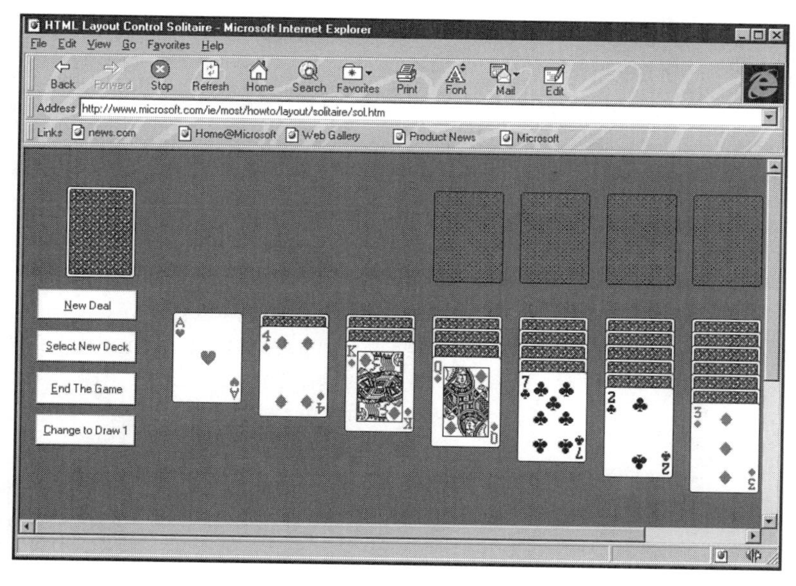

FIGURE 6. 1 Through exact placement of form elements, user interaction can exist as if the viewer was using a Windows application instead of a Web page.

Imagine you are a Web designer and have five large graphics that need to surround one larger image in an image map. Normally, there are two approaches that you can take to this situation:

- You can have your graphics designer create one image that encompasses all six of the graphics that you have.
- You can create a complex HTML table that presents the graphics arranged in a pattern that makes sense to viewers.

Through HTML layout however, you can actually place your large image on a page and then arrange the other graphics around it, anywhere you want them to appear, by selecting the different images and moving them with the mouse. Figure 6.2 shows how graphics can be arranged through HTML Layout.

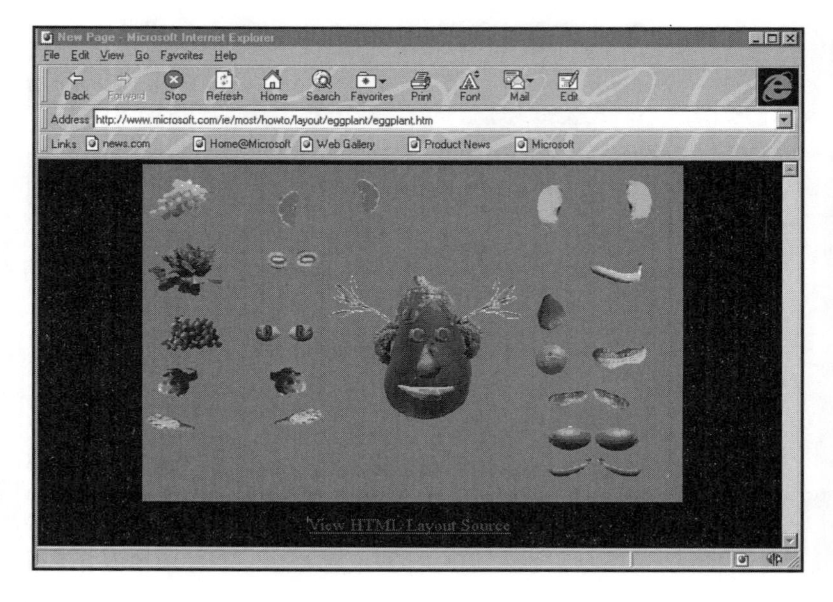

FIGURE 6. 2 Arranging graphics the way that you want them to look on-screen is now a real possibility with HTML Layout.

With HTML Layout, you can also control the order in which graphics appear and even layer and overlap images. As in most graphics programs, HTML Layout allows you to manipulate the placement of graphics as they appear on-screen. What this means is that if you have Image #1 on top of Image #2, you can select the first image and use the Move to Back command, which brings Image #2 to the front. This is useful when working with a large number of graphics that appear near each other. Overlapping graphics are demonstrated in Figure 6.3.

You can also create objects, such as toolbars, with HTML layout that can be used within a variety of Web pages with only one unique line of HTML code in each Web page. This option has been available before through server-side includes, but many Web servers did not offer this option, limiting what Web developers could do.

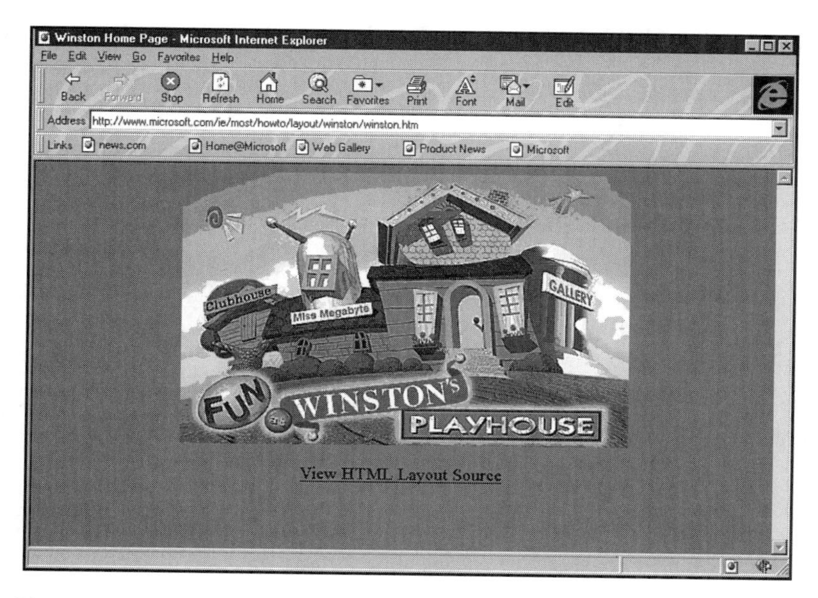

FIGURE 6. 3 By controlling the order in which overlaid graphics appear, you can create interesting visual effects.

Server-side Includes Until HTML Layout and complicated server scripts, the only way to incorporate like components into multiple pages was to use SSI. Server-side includes are referenced in your HTML page as a file, read from the server and then placed into Web pages. Though this is like HTML Layout, not all servers support SSI, whereas HTML Layout is server independent.

Figure 6.4 demonstrates how a Web site can benefit from a uniform navigation bar that will appear on every page.

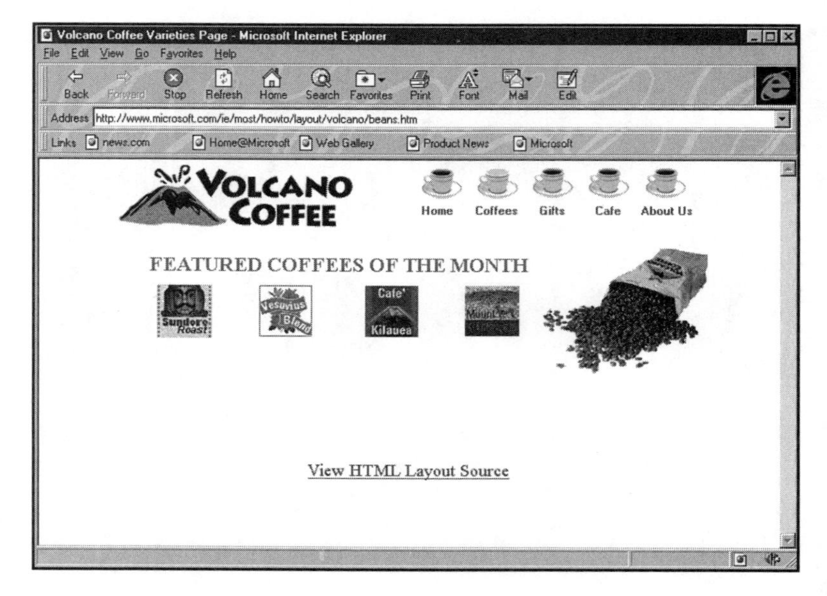

FIGURE 6. 4 Giving your Web site a uniform look with toolbars and HTML Layout capabilities enhances your viewer's experience and makes it easier for him or her to navigate your content.

Microsoft has created a Web site dedicated to displaying sites that use HTML Layout. This site can be found at **http://www.microsoft.com/workshop/author/layout/samples.htm**. Some of these sites are described in the following list.

- Planet FX **http://www.imagefx.com/planetfx/pfxdemo1.htm**

  Designed as a showcase for displaying available custom ActiveX controls. Uses HTML Layout for organizing content into a two-window site. Window panes change to new control content when clicked.

- ActiveX Solitaire **http://www.microsoft.com/ie/most/howto/layout/solitaire/sol.htm**

Advanced use of HTML Layout to display cards. This online game is exactly like playing Solitaire in Windows. View the source code for an example of extensive HTML Layout and VBScript programming.

- Mr. ActiveX Eggplant Head **http://www. microsoft. com/ie/most/howto/layout/eggplant/ eggplant.htm**

  It's the classic Mr. Potato Head with a twist—it's online. This Web page utilizes individual vegetable components that can be manipulated onto the potato with mouse actions. As you play around, notice how the layers of graphics are used when stacking multiple items in the same location.

- Winston's Playhouse **http://www.microsoft.com/ ie/most/howto/layout/winston/winston.htm**

  This entire Web site uses HTML Layout to display graphics on every Web page. This is a great example of graphics being perfectly arranged for good visual balance.

- ActiveX Minesweeper **http://www.microsoft.com/ ie/most/howto/layout/minesweeper/ minesweeper.htm**

  This site is a good example of using layered graphics. Each grey button that you click reveals another portion of the overall game board underneath. This game plays just like the Windows version.

Downloading Layout Pages Because most of the Web pages in the previous list are graphic intensive, some may take quite a while to load. If you give the Web pages a chance to fully download, however, you will be amazed at what some of the authors have done with these Web sites.

SUPPORTED BROWSERS

At this time, there is only one Web browser that supports HTML Layout, Internet Explorer 3.0 for Windows 95 and Windows NT. This should not deter you away from experimenting with HTML Layout however. Netscape Communications has recently announced that it will also be supporting HTML Layout in the next release of Netscape Navigator.

Netscape Navigator Netscape Communications was founded by the creator of NCSA Mosaic, the first Web browser. Netscape Navigator was the first Internet browser to have special HTML tags, use scripting languages, and use software plug-ins to enhance Web sites. Netscape is currently in its third release and is available on over 15 computer platforms.

Netscape's interpretation of HTML Layout will most likely be different than Microsoft's. As the browser war heats up, Netscape will probably try to better Microsoft's solution by making it easier to implement HTML Layout, which will, in turn, confuse existing users of Internet Explorer and ActiveX Control Pad by creating a second specification for the technology.

There is one way to get the functionality of HTML Layout with Netscape Navigator right now. The ScriptActive plug-in by Ncompass allows all ActiveX controls to run inside of Navigator, and provides a way for VBScript elements to function also. To download a copy of ScriptActive, point your Web browser to **http://www.ncompasslabs.com/products/scriptactive.htm**.

Microsoft has submitted their proposal to the IETF for review and acceptance. Once the proposal becomes a standard, many Web browsers will incorporate HTML Layout into their design, though a situation could arise where the interpretations differ slightly like the interpretation of HTML does today.

What is the IETF? The IETF (Internet Engineering Task Force) is responsible for reviewing proposals for standards on the Internet and implementing if approved. They are an open-body group made up of companies and individuals from all over the world. Their Web site is located at **http://www.ietf.cnri.reston.va.us/home.html**.

In this lesson, you learned what HTML Layout is for and the endless possibilities that it offers for designing visually exciting Web pages. In the next lesson, you create an HTML Layout from scratch with the help of ActiveX Control Pad.

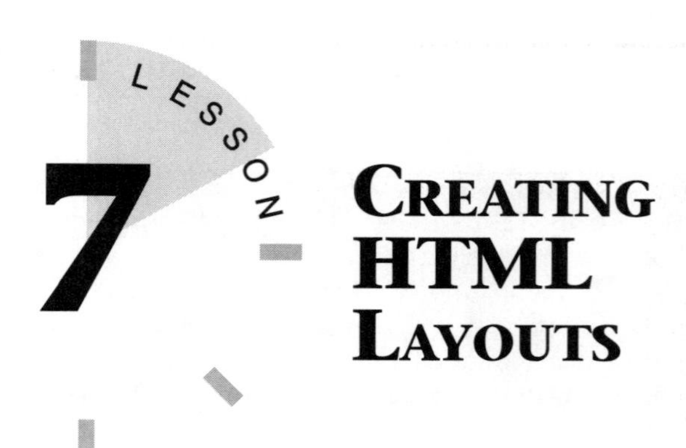

Creating HTML Layouts

In this lesson, you learn how to create a new HTML Layout, become familiar with the Toolbox controls, and add a layout to your Web pages.

Creating a New HTML Layout

Now that you know what an HTML Layout page can do, it's time to start creating your own. Creating a layout page is very easy to do with the ActiveX Control Pad. All of the basic ActiveX controls that you use in your layout pages are at your disposal through the use of the Toolbox. The Toolbox offers the ActiveX controls in a point-and-click fashion, much like adding formatting to documents in a word processor.

To create a new HTML Layout page, follow these steps:

1. Start the ActiveX Control Pad. The Control Pad opens with a blank HTML page displayed.
2. Click File, New HTML Layout. A blank HTML Layout form appears as well as the Toolbox from which you can add ActiveX controls to your layout page. Figure 7.1 illustrates a blank HTML Layout form.

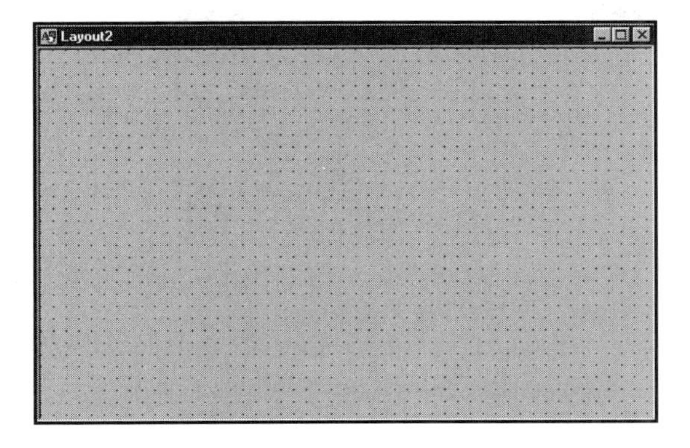

FIGURE 7. 1 Though the layout control page appears empty, it contains a vast amount of potential when creating documents that must have absolute formatting of graphics and text.

USING THE TOOLBOX

The Toolbox, as well as the controls contained within, look very familiar to Visual Basic programmers. This is almost the exact set of tools used when building forms in Visual Basic applications. As you pass your mouse over each of the controls contained within the Toolbox, the control's name pops up. This is very helpful when you are unsure of the function of the control.

I don't see a pop-up menu! Hold your mouse cursor over the button that you want information on for about 2–3 seconds. After a few moments, the pop-up message will appear, giving you the full name of the ActiveX control.

The Toolbox consists of two tabbed boxes that contain ActiveX controls. The Standard Controls tab displays the controls that are standard to every Windows system. Figure 7.2 displays all of the controls contained within the Standard Controls tab.

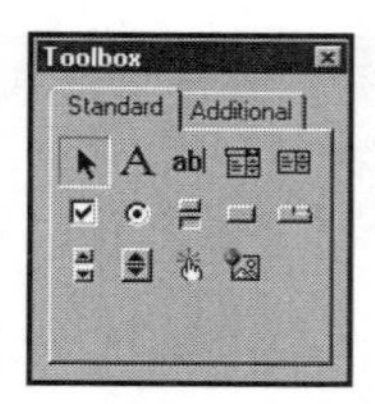

FIGURE 7.2 The Standard Controls tab contains all of the controls that are used in Windows programming.

These 13 controls allow you to create a form that can truly mimic the features found in standard Windows programs. The functions of the Standard Controls are listed below:

CONTROL	CONTROL NAME	FUNCTION
	Label	Displays a text-based label that can be any font, size, or color
	Text Box	Creates a text-entry field for user input
	Combo Box	A drop-down list from which you can access choices
	List Box	A list of choices where multiple items can be selected
	Check Box	A simple square check box for selecting a choice
	Option Button	An option button for selecting only one choice
	Toggle Button	Two-way button for selecting between two choices
	Command Button	An rectangular button for user input
	Tab Strip	Creates a tab for each item in an array of choices
	Scroll Bar	Used for scrolling information that cannot fit completely within the display window

CONTROL	CONTROL NAME	FUNCTION
	Spin Button	A dial generally used for measurement
	Hot Spot	Used for creating mouse-sensitive regions in a graphic or form
	Image	Inserts an image file into a Layout form

The Additional Controls tab, depicted in Figure 7.3, gives you access to other registered ActiveX Controls that are installed on your system. These controls will vary depending on what you have previously installed or downloaded from the Internet.

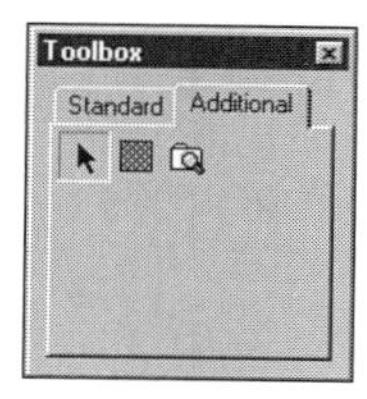

FIGURE 7.3 The Additional Controls tab allows you to incorporate non-standard ActiveX controls into your Web documents.

Over time, the controls listed under the Additional Controls tab will grow, allowing you to further enhance your HTML documents.

Adding New Controls To add a new control to the Additional Controls tab, right-click within any blank area of the tab and choose Additional Controls. You will be presented with a list of all of the ActiveX controls currently installed on your computer. Place a check in the box next to the named control that you want to add and click OK. The control will be added to the Additional Controls tab as soon as you are finished.

ADDING CONTROLS TO THE LAYOUT

Adding an ActiveX Control to your layout page is a two-part task. First, you select the control you want to use and then draw the area on the form where you want the control to appear. Use the following steps to add a Command Button to your blank Layout form:

1. Click the Command Button control on the Standard Controls tab.
2. Draw a square within the form to create a new button. Keep the button small enough so that you can add other components later. Figure 7.4 illustrates the act of resizing a control with your mouse.

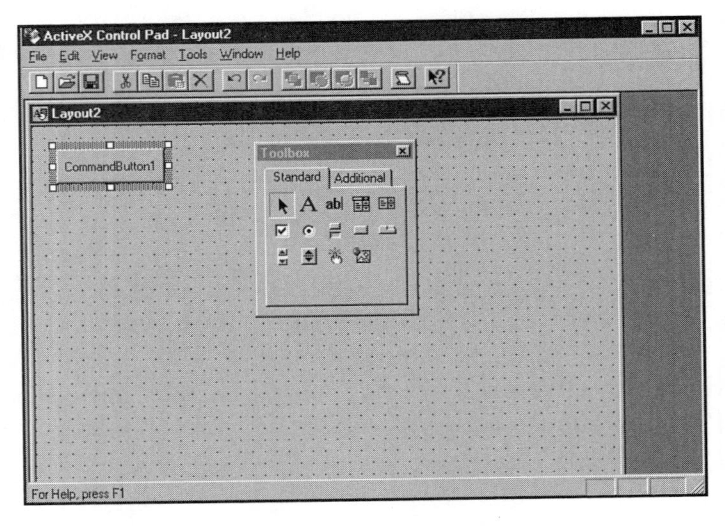

FIGURE 7.4 Placing an ActiveX Control into your Web page is much like drawing a box in a graphics program.

If you double-click the inserted ActiveX Control, the Properties window appears, listing all of the available properties of the selected control. To change the caption of the Command Button using the Properties window, follow these steps:

1. Select the Caption line within the Properties window.
2. Type **My Button** in the text box at the top of the Properties window.
3. Click Apply to make the change. Figure 7.5 shows how all of the control's properties can be edited visually.

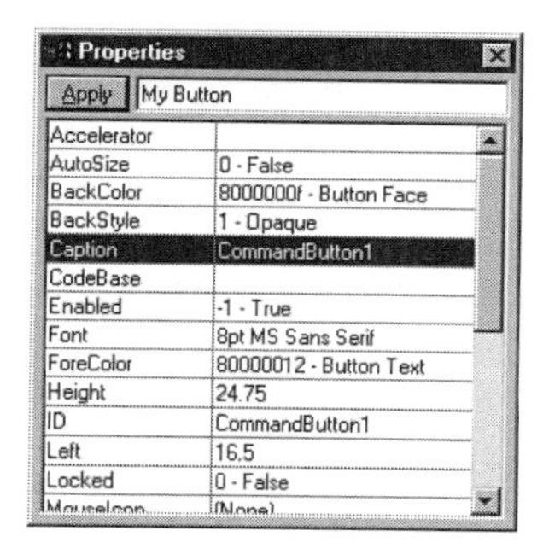

FIGURE 7.5 The Properties window allows you to change every aspect of the inserted ActiveX control.

There are many properties for each ActiveX control that you can modify. Properties such as dimension attributes, control name, caption, and color are all consistently available from the menu for customizing.

SAVING A LAYOUT

Saving your Layout page is just as easy as creating one. Choose File, Save. A standard Windows Save dialog box appears, allowing you to change the default name of the Layout page. The Control Pad's extension for a layout page is .Alx. You can actually use any file extension that you want, as long as that file is referenced in your HTML page.

Referencing an HTML Layout File For your HTML Layout file to function correctly, you must reference the specific filename within your HTML file. If you create an HTML Layout file called page.lyt, you would reference it in your HTML page with the following syntax:

```
<PARAM NAME="ALXPATH" REF
➥VALUE="file:C:\temp2\file.lyt">
```

ADDING AN HTML LAYOUT TO YOUR WEB PAGE

Now that you have created your first layout page, it is time to incorporate it into an HTML document. Since the Layout Control is just another ActiveX control itself, the control appears between `<OBJECT></OBJECT>` tags and has its own unique `CLASSID` property.

Follow these steps to insert an HTML Layout into a Web page:

1. Place your cursor within the region of the HTML page where you want the Layout Control to appear. Your Layout Control must be within the `<OBJECT></OBJECT>` tags.
2. Click Edit, Insert HTML Layout. The Insert ActiveX Control dialog box appears. Select the Layout Control that you want to insert and click OK. The Layout Control is inserted into your HTML code at the point specified by your mouse cursor in Step 1.

If you want to edit your layout page after inserting it into your HTML document, simply click the Edit HTML Layout icon to the left of the `<OBJECT></OBJECT>` tags. The layout page appears, allowing you to change any property of the inserted controls.

Save Multiple Copies of Your Work Remember that every time you save a file, you will overwrite existing files. When working with HTML Layout files, you may want to save your changes as a totally separate file, so you can revert back to a previous layout style if you do not like the one that you just completed.

In this lesson, you learned how to create an HTML Layout page, insert ActiveX controls into the page, and insert a saved layout page into an existing HTML document. In the next lesson, you learn how to insert multiple Layout Controls into one HTML file to create interesting graphic layout and effects.

Adding Multiple Layouts

In this lesson, you learn how to use multiple Layout Controls within your HTML documents to completely modify the appearance of your Web page.

Adding an Additional Layout

In the last lesson, you were introduced to the power of the HTML Layout Control. While this control works great as a stand-alone control, it really shows its power when used in conjunction with additional Layout Controls.

One advantage of using multiple Layout Controls to display your Web pages is that it is easier to modify a small portion of your Web layout rather than having to edit one document and rearrange the entire look of the page to fit your needs. For this lesson, I created a game where the user looked at three colors (a graphic), chose his or her favorite (from an ActiveX control), and submitted the data (another ActiveX control). While this example could have been built from one HTML Layout page, it makes much more sense to break it down into three distinct pages, if possible, for the ease of later editing.

My application must ultimately begin with an image displaying a few colors, for the user to choose from. The image was created with three colors, arranged side by side, and made big enough so the end user knows exactly which color he was selecting.

To create your first layout page, use the following steps:

1. Open a blank page within the Control Pad. Under the `<BODY>` tag, insert a caption for your Web page. My example used the following line of HTML:

```
<H2><FONT FACE=ARIAL>Play the Favorite
➥Color Game!</FONT></H2>
```

This line creates a title for your application using the Arial font.

2. Click File, New HTML Layout. A blank HTML Layout page appears as well as the Toolbox.

3. To adjust the `Height` property of the blank form double-click any blank space within the form itself. The Property Editor will open. Enter a numerical value. Click Apply. This resizes your form to the correct height. All three of my HTML Layout pages used a Height value of 75 pixels for a uniform feel.

4. Click the Image control within the Toolbox and draw a box into which to insert an image. This image can be any file type that is supported by Internet Explorer. Double-click the box to open the Property Editor.

What graphic formats are supported? Internet Explorer supports only GIF and JPEG files at the time of this writing.

5. Choose the `PicturePath` property from the Property Editor and type the location to your image. Click Apply. The picture fills your Image box. Resize the box if necessary to fit the image. Figure 8.1 illustrates using the Image control in HTML Layout.

6. Click File, Save to save your HTML Layout Control page. The Save dialog box will open. Enter a file name in the text box and click Save.

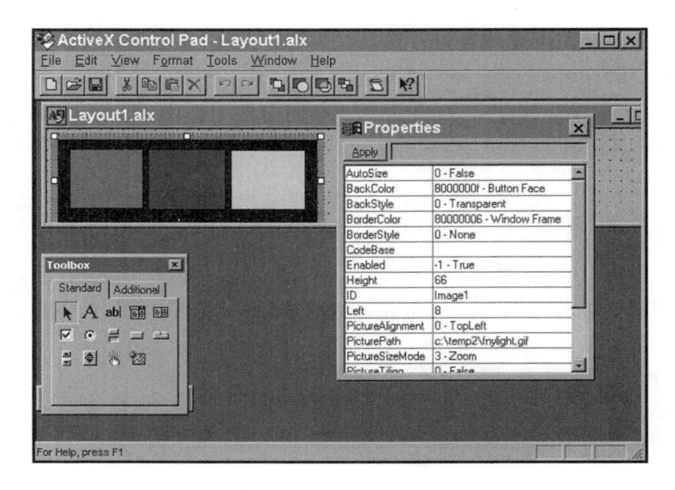

FIGURE 8.1 You can arrange images on your Web page exactly as you want them to appear with HTML Layout.

Saving Multiple Files If you are going to incorporate multiple HTML Layout files into an HTML page, it's a good idea to save your files sequentially such as layout1.alx, layout2.alx, layout3.alx, and so on. This will help you keep your layout pages in the correct order and make it easier to identify an HTML layout page that needs editing.

Now that you have your first layout element finished, it's time to create the second layout. Begin by opening a new layout file.

1. Click File, New HTML Layout to create a second layout page.
2. Double-click within the blank form to open the Property Editor. Change the `Height` property to the size that you need and click Apply.

Sizing a Control Height and Width properties are expressed in pixels only. A pixel represents one small dot on your computer screen. An easy way to know what value to use is to keep in mind that there are 72 pixels displayed per inch on a computer monitor. The interesting thing about sizing graphics, however, is the fact that many people run at high screen resolutions which can result in your graphics appearing smaller than you want them to appear. For the best results, look at all of your Web pages at different resolutions to decide how they will look best.

3. Add additional controls to complete your second layout page. For my application, I created three Option Buttons by clicking the icon in the Toolbox and drawing the buttons on the form. I sized each button so that it was big enough to contain a caption. The caption titles were changed to #1, #2, and #3, respectively, by changing the Caption property for each button. I then spread out the buttons so that they fit underneath where the different colors in my graphic appear.

4. Change the properties of any controls that need to be adjusted by double-clicking the control element. This will open the Property Editor for the respective control. Remember to click Apply to make your changes active.

5. Click File, Save and save the file in the Save dialog box. Click OK. Organizing your images with HTML Layout is illustrated in Figure 8.2.

The last step to creating my second page, was to create a Label control that would act as an instruction line for my application. The inserted label was sized so that it would match the width of my original graphic. The caption property was modified to read "What Color Is Your Favorite?" I saved the file as layout2.alx to reflect that it was the second HTML Layout file to be included in my Web page.

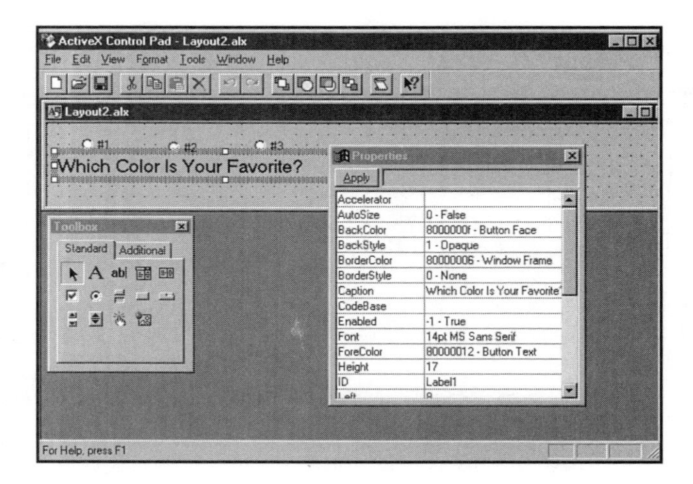

FIGURE 8.2 Organizing the physical layout of your controls is a key function of the Layout Control.

The last step to this example is to create a third layout page. In my application, layout3.alx holds two Command Button controls that act as Submit and Reset programs for my color game.

Submit and Reset Generally speaking, these buttons are used in Web pages to send form data back to the Web server and reset the entered data in case an entry error has occurred.

1. Click File, New HTML Layout to create a blank layout form.
2. Double-click a blank portion of the form to open the Property Editor. Adjust the `Height` property to the value that you need it to be. Click Apply to save your changes. My control was changed to a Height value of 50 to conserve space when the control is displayed, as shown in Figure 8.3.

3. Insert any additional controls into your layout page by selecting the icons from the Toolbox and drawing them onto the form with your mouse.

4. Double-click your controls to open the Property Editor. Adjust any properties that need to be changed within your newly inserted controls. Click Apply to retain each change to the properties.

5. Click File, Save. The Save dialog box will open. Enter a filename for your HTML Layout page and click Save.

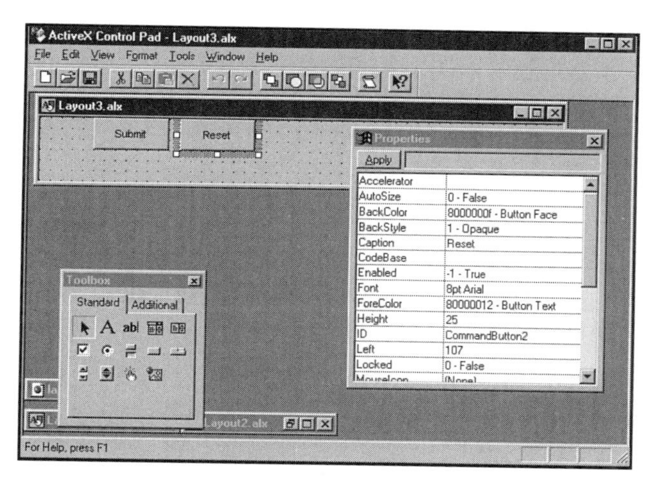

FIGURE 8.3 Using the Layout Control to incorporate buttons into your application allows you to specify exactly how they appear on-screen.

To complete my last HTML Layout page, I created two Command buttons that would act as Submit and Reset buttons. Their caption properties were adjusted to reflect their functions. The two buttons were then lined up side-by-side with the help of the form grid. The HTML Layout file was saved as layout3.alx.

What is the form grid? The HTML Layout form contains a grid that is there to assist you in lining up the components of your layout page. As you size a control with the mouse, the mouse will automatically "snap" to the grid, making it much easier for you to adjust how you want the ActiveX control to appear.

I don't have a grid! If your HTML Layout form does not display the grid, click View, Grid.

Now that all three of your layout pages are complete, you can begin incorporating your layouts into your HTML document and fine-tune the layout appearance.

ORGANIZING YOUR LAYOUTS

Since all three of your layout pages are already complete, you can now incorporate all of them into your HTML document. All three of the HTML Layout documents are placed within the HTML file, generally in order of creation. Follow these steps to complete the Layout Control Web page:

1. Click Edit, Insert HTML Layout. Choose your first HTML Layout page from the Open dialog box. The file appears in your HTML document just like any other ActiveX Control complete with a `CLASSID`.
2. Click Edit, Insert HTML Layout again. Choose your second HTML Layout page from the Open dialog box. Your second Layout Control is added to the HTML page.
3. Finally, Click Edit, Insert HTML Layout once more. Choose your last HTML Layout file from the menu. The third and last Layout Control is added to the HTML page.
4. Click File, Save. The Save dialog box will appear. Save the HTML document with a filename of your choice in the same directory as your Layout Controls.

As you analyze your HTML, your code should look similar in format to the code from my example in the following listing.

```
<HTML>
<HEAD>
<TITLE>New Page</TITLE>
</HEAD>
<BODY>
<h2><font face=arial>Play the Favorite
➥Color Game!</font></h2>

<OBJECT CLASSID="CLSID:812AE312-8B8E-11CF-
➥93C8-00AA00C08FDF"
ID="Layout1_alx" STYLE="LEFT:0;TOP:0">
<PARAM NAME="ALXPATH" REF
➥VALUE="Layout1.alx">
 </OBJECT>

<OBJECT CLASSID="CLSID:812AE312-8B8E-11CF-
➥93C8-00AA00C08FDF"
ID="Layout2_alx" STYLE="LEFT:0;TOP:0">
<PARAM NAME="ALXPATH" REF
➥VALUE="Layout2.alx">
 </OBJECT>

<OBJECT CLASSID="CLSID:812AE312-8B8E-11CF-
➥93C8-00AA00C08FDF"
ID="Layout3_alx" STYLE="LEFT:0;TOP:0">
<PARAM NAME="ALXPATH" REF
➥VALUE="Layout3.alx">

</OBJECT>
</BODY>
</HTML>
```

The concept that is really interesting here will be apparent in just a few moments when you actually view your new HTML document. You will soon understand the complexity that you can add to Web documents by just a few clicks of the mouse when authoring Layout Control pages.

TESTING YOUR LAYOUTS

The last step in developing your layout page is to actually view the page. Follow these steps to view and fine tune your new HTML page:

1. Start Internet Explorer.
2. Click File, Open. The Open dialog box will appear. Choose Browse. Locate your HTML file on your hard drive and click OK to view it. Figure 8.4 shows my game application in its finished form.

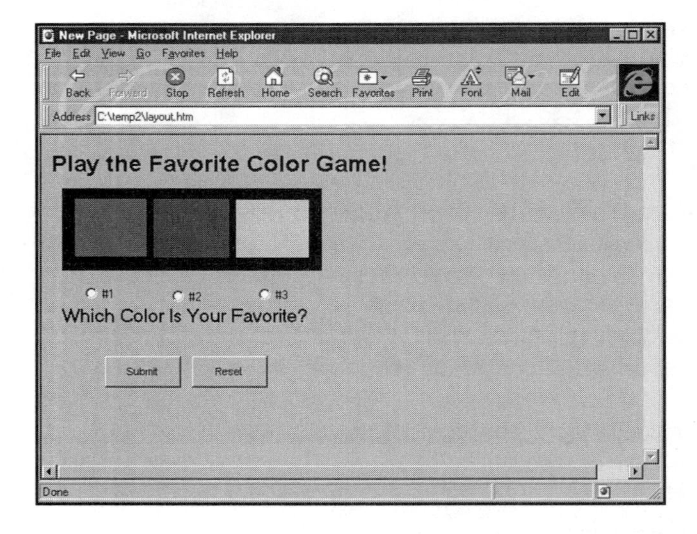

FIGURE 8.4 Incorporating multiple Layout Controls within your HTML document gives you total control as to how the elements in the page will appear.

My layouts don't appear! Make sure you inserted the HTML Layout pages into your HTML document with the Control Pad. If the control still won't load, try restarting Internet Explorer and reloading your page. Sometimes Internet Explorer's cache file doesn't work properly and the program has to completely be reloaded before pages will work.

Though your HTML page will not look like my application depicted in Figure 8.4, you will see Internet Explorer load all of the Layout Controls that you inserted. If your Layout Controls do not line up correctly, follow these tips to straighten things out:

- Remember to keep controls, such as Command buttons and Option buttons, the same size. To do this correctly every time, create the first control, and then copy and paste new copies of the control into your document. All of the controls are the same size as the first.
- Try arranging multiple Layout Controls at the same time. Figure 8.5 shows an example of viewing all three Layout Controls simultaneously to line up all of the different controls.

Arranging Controls You can resize HTML Layout windows inside of the Control Pad with the mouse as you would any other window. If your layout pages get buried under other files, you can click Window and select the file you want to use. Resize the file window and continue organizing the appearance of your page.

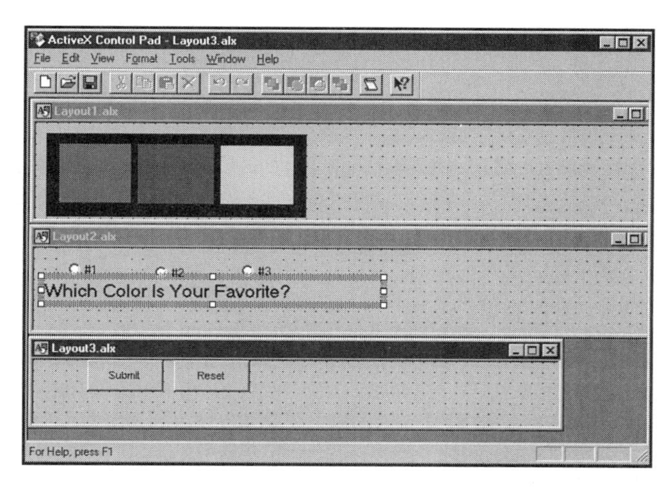

FIGURE 8.5 Viewing all of your Layout Controls at the same time allows you to line up any elements that need to be in a specific order.

In this lesson, you learned how to incorporate multiple Layout Controls into one HTML page to gain a desired look in a document. In the next lesson, you begin exploring the complexities of scripting languages and learn how they can help transition your HTML documents from static to active Web pages.

LESSON 9

Using Scripts for ActiveX Web Pages

In this lesson, you learn how using client-side scripting languages, such as VBScript and JavaScript, can help you develop interactive Web pages.

Scripting Languages: An Overview

Before the release of scripting languages, like VBScript by Microsoft and JavaScript by Netscape, the only way to provide the Web site viewer with any form of interactivity was through the use of server-side Common Gateway Interface (CGI) scripts. CGI scripts are still used today to provide such functions as forms processing and guestbook applications and must run on the same computer that the Web server is operating on. Though CGI scripts give Web pages the ability to process client information they have one definitive drawback—speed.

The order in which a CGI program is processed:

1. A signal is sent to the Web server.
2. The server initiates a response from the script.
3. The response is sent to the user.

This process might only take a few seconds, but it contributes to higher Web server process loads and can ultimately result in slowing down the Web server. Enter scripting languages.

CGI Scripts For years, the only way to incorporate interactivity into a Web page was through the use of Common Gateway Interface scripts. These scripts were run on the server and ate up valuable processor time and free memory. With the release of scripting languages, many functions that used to run on the server can now run on the client's computer, freeing up the server to only serve HTML documents.

Scripts are composed within the HTML document itself through an inline entry between the `<SCRIPT></SCRIPT>` tags. Since the scripts are downloaded as the HTML page loads, script functions are processed immediately on the client side. This opens up a huge window of opportunity for the Web programmer. Without server and speed limitations, Web pages can be made active or interactive, eventually resulting in a more pleasurable experience for the end user.

The following is a list of some Web sites incorporating scripts in creative ways:

- Fade **http://www.eto.com/JavaScript/fade/both.html**

  This site uses JavaScript to fade the background color of a Web page in and out.

- Memory **http://www.macaw.nl/teun/**

  A memory game created in JavaScript that is launched in a separate window from your browser.

- Mortgage Calculator **http://www.sni.net/~cdt/calcintro.htm**

  An online real estate company that provides a mortgage calculator written with VBScript and ActiveX controls.

- The Klicodex **http://www.ggroup.com/klicodex/index.html**

  Written in VBScript, this online Rolodex of business cards can contain your business information too.

- Schemer **http://www.coolnerds.com/vbscript/vbcolor.htm**

  This application, written entirely in VBScript, allows you to select different colors for HTML text components and then displays what the choices would look like in real-time.

- Conversion Maestro **http://www.coolnerds.com/jscript/alanconv.htm**

  Enter a weight, distance, or temperature and have this JavaScript application convert it to another form of measurement.

To access these sites in Internet Explorer, follow these steps:

1. Click File, Open. The Open dialog box will appear.
2. Type the URL as it appears in the preceding list. Click Open. The Web site that you entered will open in your Web browser.

The Web sites open so slowly. If a Web page appears to download slowly in your Web browser it is most likely either a problem with your connection to the Internet, a slow Web server sending you the document, or a Web page with a lot of HTML content or graphics. Whatever the cause, have a little patience and the sites should eventually open.

Not all Web browsers currently support scripting languages. In fact, Internet Explorer by Microsoft and Netscape Navigator are the only two browsers to support scripting. To hide scripts from browsers that cannot handle them, the scripts are contained within HTML comment tags in the following format:

```
<SCRIPT LANGUAGE='language_name'>
<!--
Script Data
-->
</SCRIPT>
```

Why do I need to hide scripts? Good question. If you do not hide your scripts within a Web page a Web browser that doesn't have scripting capabilities will simply display the contents of the script. Hiding the script makes it so that the end user will never see your script, regardless of the capabilities of the browser.

If the browser cannot understand scripts, it simply ignores the `<SCRIPT></SCRIPT>` tags. As of today, there are only two accepted scripting languages used on the Internet, VBScript and JavaScript.

To see how a script is implemented in an HTML page, follow these steps:

1. Open one of the Web sites from the list given earlier in this lesson.
2. Click View, Source. The Web page source code will open, allowing you to view how the page was composed.

When viewing the source of Web sites, pay special attention to the code contained within the `<SCRIPT></SCRIPT>` tags. Though it's impolite to steal authors' scripts, you can always view them to form your own scripting ideas.

USING VBSCRIPT

VBScript is a subset of Visual Basic, which essentially means that the syntax is the same but not all of the features are included. This was done primarily for security reasons. If a Web programmer was allowed advanced functions, such as file-system manipulation and true I/O programmability, the end user's machine could be seriously at risk. Though these features are not in place, VBScript remains a powerful programming language for manipulating ActiveX controls and changing the look of Web pages within a client browser.

I/O Programmability Being security conscious, Microsoft created VBScript with a limitation as to how powerful the language actually is. You cannot manipulate files on a hard drive with VBScript. That is, you cannot append a file on someone's computer, or gain information from a file contained on someone's computer.

Unlike the full version of Visual Basic, VBScript does not have an IDE (Integrated Development Environment). All scripts written in VBScript are composed in an ASCII text editor like HTML. To automate the process of writing scripts, however, Microsoft included the Script Wizard in the ActiveX Control Pad. Through a point-and-click interface, scripts can be built or dissected within the application. In Lesson 10, "Using the Script Wizard," you become familiar with the Script Wizard and how to include scripts in your HTML documents.

Microsoft has gone to great lengths to provide a healthy amount of documentation on VBScript in their Web site. You can access all of the online documentation and sample scripts at **http://www.microsoft.com/vbscript/**. On this site, you have access to all of VBScript's documentation on data types, variables, constants, operators, and procedures. There are also various documents covering topics such as how to reference scripts in your Web pages and how to control the program flow during design time. Figure 9.1 shows the VBScript Web site and gives you an idea of the content contained within.

Bookmark the VBScript Web Site Make sure you make an entry in your Favorites menu or Bookmarks menu for the VBScript Web site. It is updated often and you should check it for new information regularly if you are serious about programming with the VBScript language.

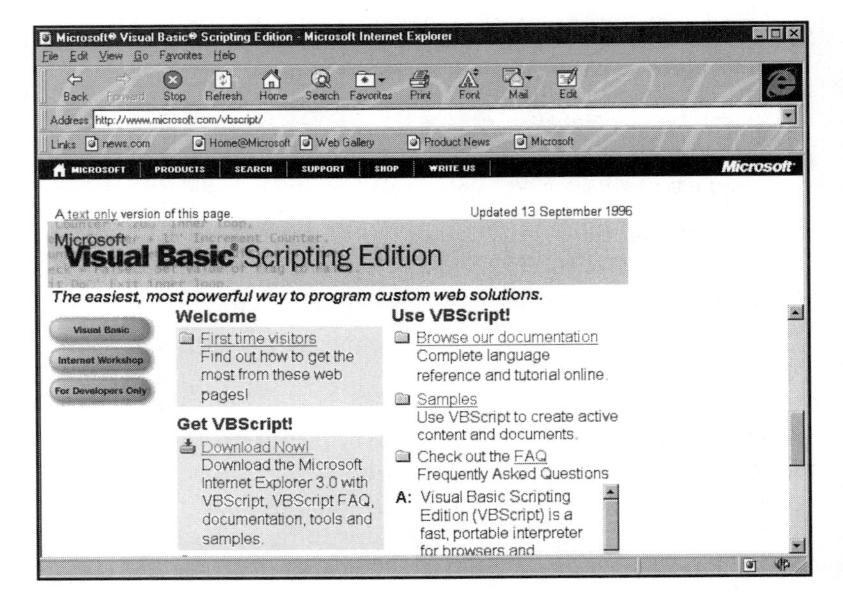

FIGURE 9.1 One of the greatest resources you can use to learn VBScript is Microsoft's Visual Basic Scripting Edition home page.

VBScript gives you not only the ability to manipulate ActiveX Controls, but Java applets as well. After dedicating some time to learning VBScript, you can create Web pages that vary in function from online games to discussion forums. Currently there is only one browser that supports VBScript upon installation, Internet Explorer. However, Netscape users can download the Ncompass ScriptActive plug-in from **http://www.ncompasslabs.com/products/scriptactive.htm**. This will allow the browser to utilize ActiveX controls and VBScript as though the function was built in.

USING JAVASCRIPT

JavaScript is a creation of Netscape Communication Corporation that was originally built into Navigator 2.0, and which marked the debut of the Java programming language in a mainstream browser. JavaScript was designed with the Java language concurrently to manipulate a Web page's appearance and to control certain aspects of Java applications. JavaScript is currently available in releases of Netscape Navigator 2.0 and Microsoft's Internet Explorer 3.0, making it a strong candidate for the standard scripting language of the WWW.

Like VBScript, all of the documentation for JavaScript is online. It can be found at **http://home.netscape.com/eng/mozilla/Gold/handbook/javascript/index.html**. Figure 9.2 shows the JavaScript Web page and the some of the content contained within.

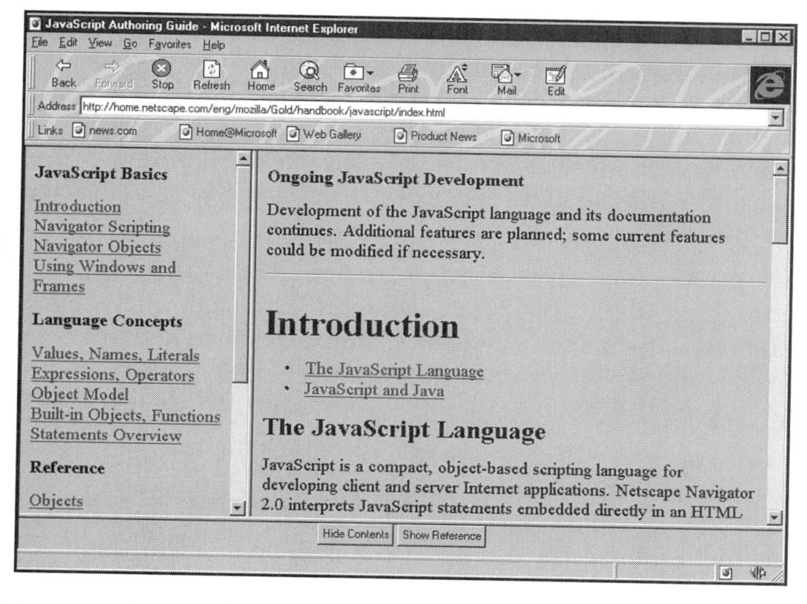

FIGURE 9.2 JavaScript's complex syntax is fully documented on Netscape Communication's Web site.

With JavaScript, Web authors have found very creative ways of incorporating new technologies such as scrolling text and browser appearance changes into their Web site. To see examples of the exciting use of JavaScript within Web pages, point your browser to **www.gamelan.com/noframe/Gamelan.javascript.html**. Gamelan's Web site is dedicated to organizing the greatest JavaScript applications on one Web site. As you view sample JavaScript uses, remember that you can always view the document source to see how something was done. Just make sure that you never reuse someone else's code directly without prior permission.

JSCRIPT

Like JavaScript, JScript was created as an Internet scripting language patterned after Java. In fact, JScript and JavaScript are essentially the same scripting language with only a few differences. Microsoft created JScript after JavaScript, but with enhancements to the language for accessing ActiveX controls as well as Java applets. This was a good idea since ActiveX did not exist when JavaScript was created by Netscape Communications. Now, programmers can use a Java-based scripting language to access ActiveX objects and Java applets without having to mix languages on different Web pages.

The JScript home page is located at **http://www.microsoft.com/jscript**. This Web site provides a great wealth of information on JScript language reference, sample applications, and hosting JScript in custom software programs.

The downside to the JScript language is that only Internet Explorer supports it. In addition, the language itself is still in beta testing and looks to remain so for some time. If you are developing a Web site that is designed to be viewed exclusively in Internet Explorer, you can use JScript with no problem. But if your target audience is the entire Internet, and all of its browsers, you are better off going with a widely accepted scripting language like JavaScript.

WHICH SCRIPTING LANGUAGE IS RIGHT FOR YOU?

One of the hardest choices that Web developers face today is which scripting language to use when creating applications. Though VBScript and JavaScript can do many of the same functions, there are some definite advantages and disadvantages to each.

Currently, VBScript is only supported without additional components, such as ScriptActive, in Internet Explorer 3.0. This means that the majority of Web surfers on the Internet today do not have access to your scripts because Netscape Navigator remains the most widely used browser. Internet Explorer is gaining popularity, though. Because Internet Explorer can be obtained free of charge, many users are making the switch.

It is up to you whether or not you compose two sets of applications for the two different browsers. Most of the time, that will not be the popular attitude, and you could find yourself wishing that you picked JavaScript exclusively.

One advantage that VBScript does have is the fact that is based upon a programming language that has been around for five years and has generated over two million Visual Basic programmers. Most of these programmers can look over the rules for VBScript for a short period of time and then begin scripting right away. It is also the language most tightly integrated with ActiveX controls and the Windows platform itself, meaning that if you plan on quite a bit of ActiveX content, you'll probably want to stick with VBScript. While JScript also has built in "hooks" for ActiveX controls, most beginning programmers will find VBScript much easier to learn.

On the other hand, JavaScript, resembling Java so closely, presents a tough learning curve for beginning and experienced programmers. Those experienced in Java and C programming, however, will have a much easier time learning the scripting language. JavaScript is very new and changes frequently, resulting in a more streamlined and effective language. This can lead to some browsers interpreting the scripts correctly, while others may not be able to access it at all.

The choice is up to you. Become familiar with both languages and choose the one that is right for the application you are developing. You might find that the time you spend developing your scripts is divided evenly between both languages.

In this lesson, you learned about the similarities and differences between scripting languages and how they can be used within your Web pages. In the next lesson, you become familiar with the Script Wizard to develop scripts quickly and easily.

USING THE SCRIPT WIZARD

In this lesson, you learn what the purpose of the Script Wizard is and how to navigate its sometimes complex interface.

WHAT IS THE SCRIPT WIZARD?

When Microsoft designed ActiveX Control Pad, they knew that not everyone using it would be a programmer. They wanted to build extensibility into the product so that even the beginning Webmaster could use ActiveX controls to bring life to his or her Web site. With this in mind, Microsoft built a Script Wizard with a point-and-click interface to complete VBScript or JavaScript code listings.

Though neither of these scripting languages are easy to learn unless you have prior programming experience, the point-and-click interface is a great introduction to events, actions, and procedures.

RUNNING THE SCRIPT WIZARD

To access the Script Wizard, follow these steps:

1. Click Tools, Script Wizard.
2. Alternatively, you can click the Script Wizard icon on the right side of the toolbar.

The Script Wizard appears, displaying the various panes and command buttons. Figure 10.1 demonstrates how the Script Wizard will look when you first open it.

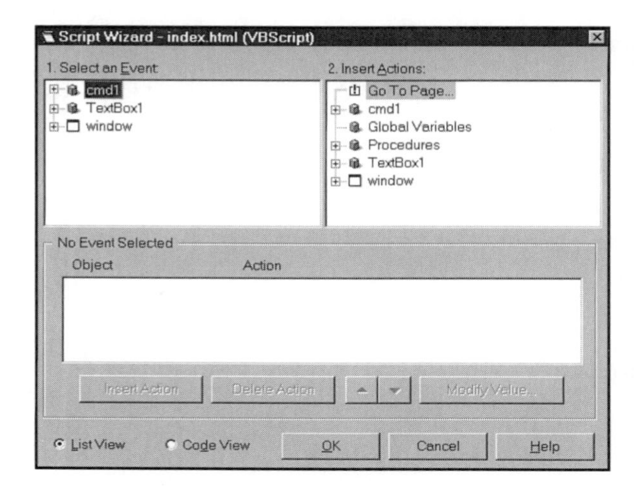

FIGURE 10.1 The Script Wizard is a simple point-and-click interface to interactive Web programming.

The type of scripting language used by ActiveX Control Pad is VBScript. If you prefer your scripts to be in JavaScript, click Tools, Options, Script and choose the scripting language that you prefer.

The left pane of the Script Wizard is called the Event pane and contains all the events within your Web page. Events encompass any action that can lead to a response. Two examples of events are a mouse click on a button or scrolling down a slider bar.

The right pane is the Action pane. An action is a direct result of an event. Changes in a button color or the sound of a door slamming when a Web page is exited are examples of actions. Global variables and procedures are also controlled in the Action pane.

The Script pane is the pane at the bottom of the Script Wizard. The Script pane contains event handlers for each action assigned to an event. The script that eventually causes your page to come alive is listed within the Script pane.

Event Handlers An event handler is the actual code that is used when deciding what happens when an event occurs. If you had a Label control that changed its caption property when clicked, the VBScript event handler would look like the following example.

```
<SCRIPT LANGUAGE="VBScript">
<!--
Sub Label1_Click()
Label1.Caption = "Second caption"
end sub
-->
  </SCRIPT>
```

If you are familiar with scripting languages, you may want to change the view of the Script pane to Code View, which you can do from the bottom of the Script Wizard. This allows you to edit code directly. You are able to switch back and forth at any time so that your scripting techniques are as effective as possible. The Insert Action and Delete Action buttons can be used at any time to create an event handler in your script. You can also use the arrow buttons on the right side to organize your script events so that they happen in the correct order.

ADDING EVENTS TO YOUR CONTROLS

Until you add an ActiveX Control to your Web page, your event usage will be limited. That's not to say that it's useless. The core of Internet Explorer is an ActiveX Control itself and it's the control's events that can be used to trigger actions. Through Internet Explorer's built-in events such as `onLoad` (opening a page) and `onUnload` (leaving a page), you can create an active Web page without inserting additional controls at all.

All of a control's events are listed in the Event window inside of the Script Wizard. Every event listed has an empty diamond to the left of the event name that informs you that this is, in fact, an event and can be used to initiate actions. Once you have associated an action with an event, the diamond will become solid black in color, showing that it has been used.

If you expand the Window property by clicking the plus sign in the Event window, you will notice the two events `onLoad` and `onUnload`. These events are equal to the browser window opening a document and unloading a Web document (or moving on to the next). Later, when you become familiar with actions and how they relate to events, you can control every function of the Web browser, from accessing the History list to controlling the appearance of frames for a frame-capable browser.

To add an event to your Web page, follow these steps:

1. Click File, New HTML to generate an HTML template page.
2. Click Tools, Script Wizard. The Script Wizard will open listing only one item whose events you can use, the Window. The Window represents the area that displays Web pages in your Web browser.
3. Click the plus sign next to Window to drop down the list of available events. The two events available to this object, `onLoad` and `unLoad`, will appear in the list.
4. Highlight the `onLoad` event. This will make `onLoad` the active event.
5. Double-click Go To Page to bring up the Go To Page dialog box. Type **http://www.news.com** into the text box and click OK. The event `onLoad` now has an action associated with it and the VBScript code will be generated in your HTML page.
6. Click OK to insert the code into your Web page.

OnLoad The onLoad event occurs as soon as the window loads a new object. This object does not necessarily need to be an HTML page. It can also be a single image, a sound file, or an animation. When an action is associated to the onLoad event, it will take place as soon as the browser begins loading its content.

Once your code is inserted, your HTML page should look like the following:

```
<HTML>
<HEAD>
    <SCRIPT LANGUAGE="VBScript">
<!--
Sub window_onLoad()
Window.location.href = "http://
➥www.news.com/index.html"
end sub
-->
    </SCRIPT>
<TITLE>New Page</TITLE>
</HEAD>
<BODY>
</BODY>
</HTML>
```

When you save your Web page and load it into Internet Explorer, as soon as the page begins to load it will immediately begin loading the home page of Cnet's News Web site.

Using the Same Event Multiple Times There is no limit to the amount of times you can use an event in a Web page. This is useful when you want a variety of actions to occur when the user clicks something. You can actually have a single control on your Web page that a user clicks, that will result in the page changing all of its colors, playing a sound, and making a new ActiveX control appear. To add another action to an event, simply double-click the event name that you wish to use again and choose an appropriate action in the Action pane.

USING ACTIONS

Actions are listed in the Action pane as a value that can be manipulated through an event. To assign an action to an event within the Script Wizard, use the following steps:

1. Select the event that you want to reference in the Event pane.
2. Double-click the appropriate action in the Action pane. The action window appears, prompting you for a string or text to use as reference.

Global variables and procedures can also be accessed from within the Action pane. These are assigned through your code in the Code View. Global variables are simply values that you want to have access to from your entire site in the case of Web development. Procedures are pieces of code that can be reused for the same function in different areas. This is more useful and efficient than re-entering code that you've used before.

Global Variables A global variable is a variable that can be accessed and changed by any event used in a Web site. To insert a global variable into your Web page, right-click in the Action pane of the Script Wizard and choose New Global Variable. Type a name into the New Global Variable dialog box and click OK. Now, when you click the plus sign next to Global Variables in the Action pane, your variable will be there and you can associate it to any available event.

INSERTING SCRIPT INTO YOUR HTML

When adding script elements through the Script Wizard, the script components and ActiveX controls are automatically inserted into your HTML page. If you want to go back and edit existing scripts, simply click the Edit Script icon, as shown in Figure

10.2, next to the inserted code. The Script Wizard will open with the appropriate event and action displayed.

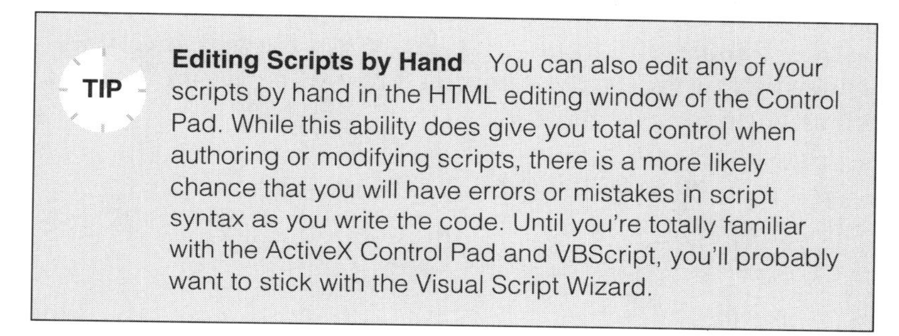

Editing Scripts by Hand You can also edit any of your scripts by hand in the HTML editing window of the Control Pad. While this ability does give you total control when authoring or modifying scripts, there is a more likely chance that you will have errors or mistakes in script syntax as you write the code. Until you're totally familiar with the ActiveX Control Pad and VBScript, you'll probably want to stick with the Visual Script Wizard.

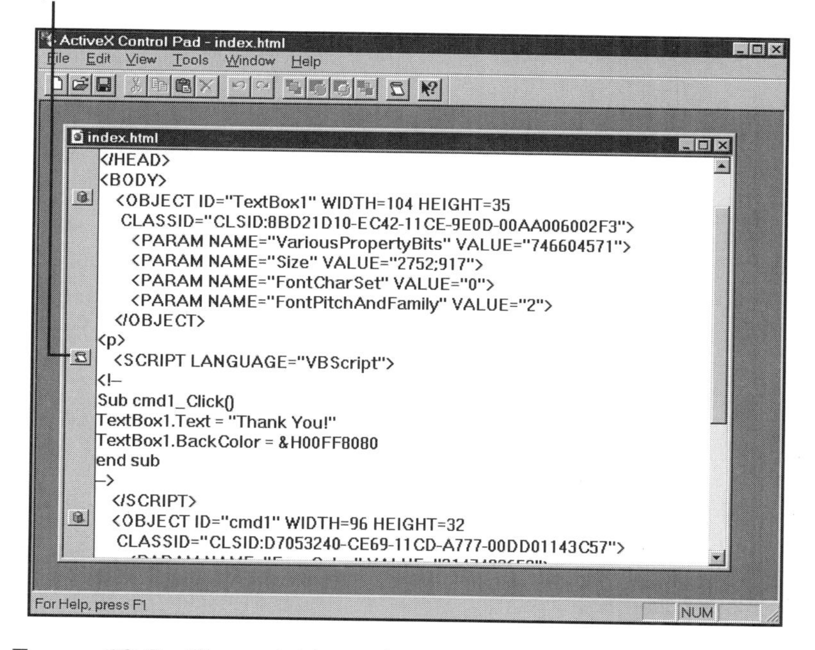

FIGURE 10.2 The script icon gives you one-click access to the Script Wizard to edit existing snippets of code.

Opening an existing script in the Script Wizard displays all of your actions within the Script pane for you to edit.

In this lesson, you learned how to open the Script Wizard and became familiar with its physical makeup. In the next lesson, you will insert your first ActiveX control into a Web page and activate it with VBScript.

Using the Popup Menu Control

In this lesson, you learn how to insert a Popup Menu Control into a Web page making navigation of different sources of content as easy as choosing from a simple menu.

Using the Popup Menu as Navigation

Before ActiveX controls graced the Web, many people used frames to navigate Web sites. Frames allowed users to navigate around a Web site, with a site directory that was always visible in one frame. The one problem navigating with frames is that the browser window is generally still cluttered with links that may confuse the end user.

One of the ActiveX controls that is included with Internet Explorer 3.0 is the Popup Menu Control. This control presents the user with one button from which a number of choices can pop out for selection. In the following steps, you create a Popup Menu that presents a list of five sources for news on the Internet.

1. Begin by creating a new page in ActiveX Control Pad.
2. Click Edit, Insert ActiveX Control. From the Insert ActiveX Control dialog box, choose Microsoft IE 30 Popup Menu Control. Click OK.

This control is interesting because the functionality lies within the VBScript code, not the properties of the control itself. This simply means that the control itself will do nothing. You must insert a few lines of VB Script code to make the control work.

ADDING FUNCTIONALITY TO THE CONTROL

The targets of your Popup control are listed as `Menuitems` in the Property Editor. As you look at the properties of the control, a field for `Menuitems` appears, though nothing you type into that field is retained. The `Menuitem` property is not designed to handle multiple choices. This is a placeholder for future VBScript code that you will insert.

Menuitem Each item that you want to appear when the user clicks your Popup control is listed as Menuitem in your script. The Property Editor does not have the ability to add Menuitems, so you must insert them as parameters within the `<OBJECT></OBJECT>` tags. Each Menuitem must appear in your script in the order that it will appear in the Popup menu. Each individual item is assigned an ID number between brackets that will be used by further VBScript code to make each selected item do something.

To create Menuitems for your five news sources you will need to enter the information directly into your Web page. Remember to close the Property Editor and Edit ActiveX Control window so that you can type in the body of the HTML page.

1. Enter the following code before the `</OBJECT>` tag in your HTML page:

```
<PARAM NAME="Menuitem[0]" value="The Wall
➥Street Journal">
<PARAM NAME="Menuitem[1]" value="USA
➥Today">
<PARAM NAME="Menuitem[2]" value="The
➥Dallas Morning News">
<PARAM NAME="Menuitem[3]" value="The New
➥York Times">
<PARAM NAME="Menuitem[4]"
➥value="News.com">
```

2. Create a button that represents your Popup menu by inserting the following code into your HTML page below the </OBJECT> tag:

```
<INPUT TYPE="button" NAME="ShowMenu"
➥VALUE="Sources for News" ALIGN=RIGHT>
```

Now it's time to make your control come alive with some VBScript code. Since you've already assigned a value to each of the Menuitems, it's easy to call each one and associate an URL for the Web browser to move to. Your script will be placed just below your ActiveX control in the HTML page.

Follow these steps to add functionality to your Popup Menu control:

1. Type the following statement into the body of your HTML page, below the button that you just inserted.

```
<SCRIPT Language="VBScript">
<!---
Sub Iepop1_Click(ByVal Menuitem )
```

Now you must add a Case statement that defines the target of each Menuitem associated by number.

2. Add a Case statement by typing the following code under the script elements that you just inserted.

```
Select Case Menuitem
     Case 1
          Window.location.href = "http:/
➥/www.wsj.com/index.html"
     Case 2
          Window.location.href = "http://
➥www.usatoday.com/index.html"
     Case 3
          Window.location.href = "http://
➥www.dallasnews.com/index.html"
```

```
        Case 4
             Window.location.href = "http://
➥www.nyt.com/index.html"
        Case 5
             Window.location.href = "http://
➥www.news.com/index.html"
```

The first line of the script tells the browser what scripting language is being used within the HTML document. The second line states that the Popup Menu Control (Iepop1) will appear and selects the appropriate numerical value of the `Menuitem`. The remaining portion of the script allows each choice listed to have an associated value through the use of the `Case` statement.

Case The `Case` statement is used when referring to a list of items being accessed, like the choices in the Popup control. Each case line states the ID assigned to an individual choice in the Popup list and assigns a value to that choice.

The next step is to close the `Sub` procedure with the following code:

```
End Select
End Sub
```

The last step is a subroutine that calls the Popup Menu Control when the `ShowMenu` button is clicked. Insert the following code to close the script:

```
Sub ShowMenu_onClick
    Call Iepop1.Popup
End Sub
--!>
</SCRIPT>
```

Figure 11.1 demonstrates the Popup Menu Control in action.

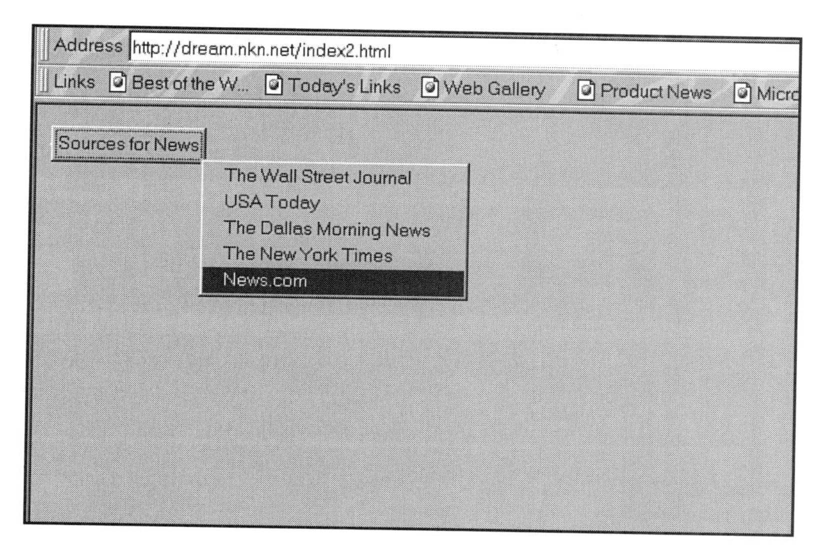

FIGURE 11.1 The Popup Menu Control is a handy way of reducing screen clutter while offering an easy navigation tool.

What is a Sub? Sub is short for subroutine. A subroutine is a portion of a script whose contents are contained between the statements Sub and End Sub. You can think of a subroutine as something that happens as a result of an action. In the case of the previous sample application, the subroutine is run when the event onClick is triggered. The Sub function runs while the rest of the script is processing the Popup menu, and enables the Popup menu to have a value when clicked.

ACCESSING THE POPUP MENU'S METHODS

Although there are no properties to change or events to trigger from the Popup Menu, the control does have quite a few distinct methods that can be utilized.

Method A method is a statement within VBScript code that processes an action for a specific object. For example, if you wanted a new Menuitem to be generated when the user double-clicked the Popup Menu Control, you could create a method that adds a new choice to the menu. The code would look like the following:

```
Iepopup1.menuitem[6}="Infoworld"
```

The following table displays a summary of the methods associated with the Popup control.

TABLE 11.1 METHODS OF THE POPUP MENU

METHOD NAME	FUNCTION
`Popup`	Generates the Popup window; contains the following parameters:
`Scale`	True/False value
`True`	Scales the content to fit within the Popup menu
`False`	Crops the content to fit within the Popup menu
`URL`	The location of the page to be displayed
`Dismiss`	Kills the current Popup window
`AboutBox`	Displays the About dialog box

I don't have the same methods listed! Different versions of the standard Microsoft ActiveX controls are updated often, resulting in many releases of the same file. You might have an earlier version of the control which has a limited list of methods, or a later version that contains many more methods. Regardless, you will be able to download the most current version at **http://www.microsoft.com/activex/gallery/**.

You find, however, that most of the functionality of the Popup Menu Control is within the listings of the `Menuitem` and the `Case...select` statements.

Save the work that you have completed up until this point and open it within Internet Explorer. After you have the page working fully, experiment by adding your own menuitems and values to create a customized navigational tool.

To see an advanced use of the Popup Menu Control in action, point your Web browser to **http://www.microsoft.com/ntserver/default.asp**. This page is a combination of server- and client-side scripting to achieve nested menus. Tackle this one only if you dare lose sleep!

In this lesson, you learned how add a Popup Menu Control to a Web page to access a variety of choices from one button. In the next lesson, you learn how to use the Command Button ActiveX Control to change another control's properties.

LESSON 12

Using the Command Button Control

In this lesson, you learn how to insert a Command Button Control into your Web page and pick up some tips as to what can be achieved with the ActiveX Control.

Using the Command Button Control to Change Object Properties

The Command Button Control is really the simplest control to utilize in a Web document. Think of the Command Button as a trigger for any event that can happen within a Web browser. Using the Command Button Control, you can develop the basis for interactive applications: that is, a Web page whose look the user can actually control by clicking buttons.

You might use this control as an alternative button for submitting a form, changing the content within a Web browser, or navigating your site with a system of custom controls. Using the Command Button Control, which allows you to use the same control to display the buttons in your Web browser as your installed Windows applications do, can give your Web documents the appearance of real Windows-based applications.

In this lesson, we're actually going to be using two controls, the Command Button Control and the Text Box Control, both of which are installed on your system when the ActiveX Control Pad is installed.

1. Click File, New HTML or Ctrl+N to create a blank Web document.
2. Place your cursor anywhere within the `<BODY></BODY>` tags to insert your first ActiveX Control.
3. Click Edit, Insert ActiveX Control. The Insert ActiveX Control dialog box appears. From the list, choose Microsoft Forms 2.0 Text Box.
4. Close the Edit ActiveX Control window. You will not be changing this control at all.
5. Type **<P>** after the `</OBJECT>` tag. This inserts a double-line break between controls once the second control is inserted.
6. Click Edit, Insert ActiveX Control. The Insert ActiveX Control dialog box appears. Choose Microsoft Forms 2.0 Command Button from the list of ActiveX controls.
7. Close the Edit ActiveX Control window once more.

Within your HTML code you have now defined two ActiveX Controls that are working components when your page is published on the Web server. At this point, if the page is accessed within a Web browser, the page loads the controls, but nothing happens if you click the Command Button. In fact, the page as it stands right now is quite boring to look at. Figure 12.1 illustrates an inserted ActiveX control that does nothing.

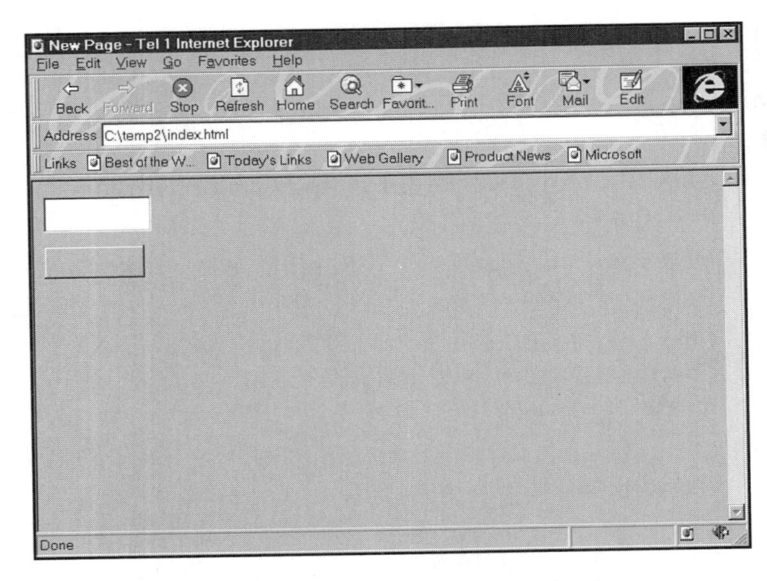

FIGURE 12.1 Inserting ActiveX Controls is a simple process.

Now that the two controls are placed into the Web page correctly, it's time to manipulate the appearance of the components.

USING THE COMMAND BUTTON CONTROL PROPERTIES

Editing the properties of any ActiveX Control can be done at two different times. You can choose to change the properties as soon as you add the control to your page or after the initial page layout is set. In this example, you are changing the properties after the page layout is complete.

1. Click the Edit ActiveX Control button located to the left of Command Button Control within the HTML document. The Properties window appears, allowing you to modify the control as shown in Figure 12.2.

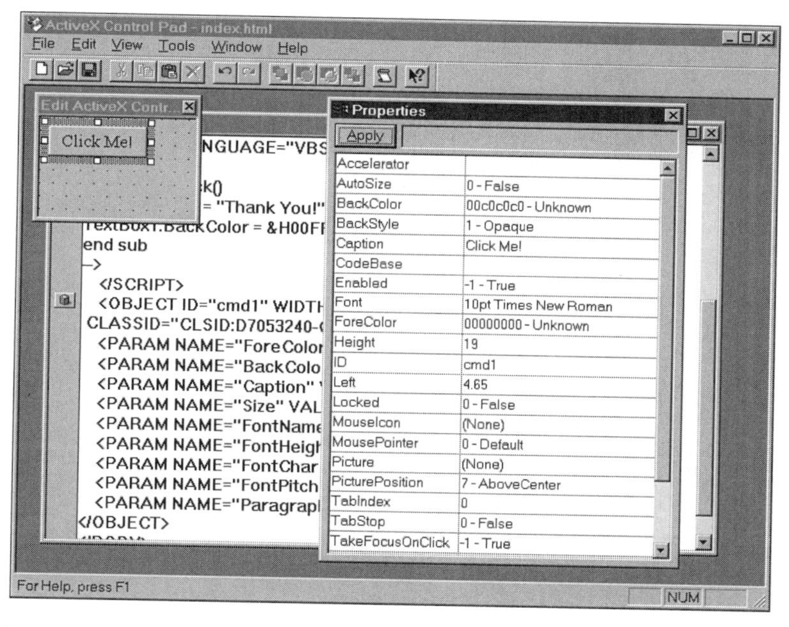

FIGURE 12.2 The properties of the Command Button Control change the appearance of the button in regards to look, color, and other special options, such as the appearance of the mouse pointer as it passes over.

2. Click within the `ID` property and delete the existing text. Type **cmd1** in the blank field above the list of properties. Click Apply to save your changes. This shortens the name of the command button for later easy reference.

Highlight the `Caption` property and type **Click Me!** in the blank field. Click Apply. The caption of the command button changes to reflect its new caption.

Click within the `Font` property and change the value to 10pt Times New Roman. Click Apply to view your changes.

Close the Properties window and the Edit Active Control box. Click the Save button on the toolbar to save your changes. Figure 12.3 demonstrates the changed `Caption` property of the control.

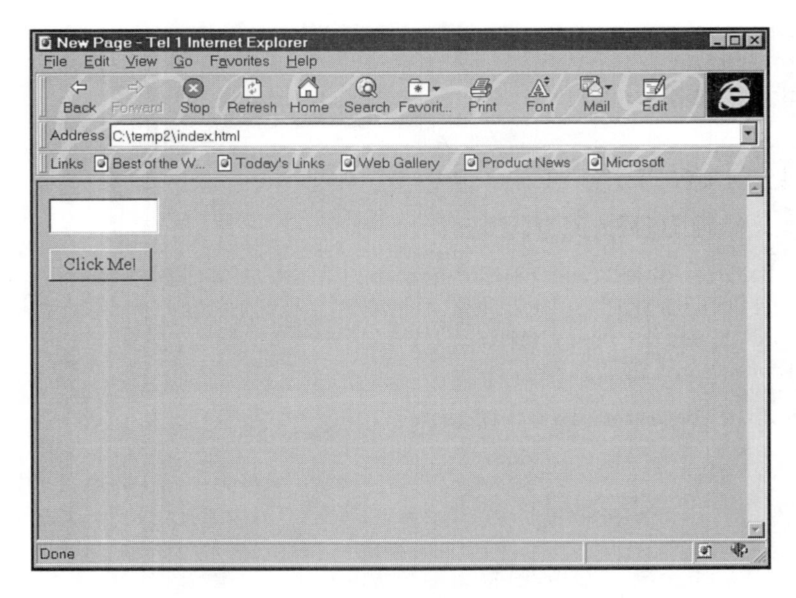

FIGURE 12.3 The command button receives a new caption.

A few other useful properties of the Command Button Control are listed in Table 12.1.

TABLE 12.1 COMMAND BUTTON PROPERTIES

PROPERTY NAME	FUNCTION
`BackColor`	Changes the background appearance of the button or text
`ForeColor`	Modifies the foreground appearance of the button component
`Enabled`	Controls the functionality of the command button like an On/Off switch
`MousePointer`	Changes the appearance of the mouse pointer as the cursor is passed over the control
`Picture`	Allows the command button to display a graphic instead of text

Now that you have modified the appearance of your control, it's time to make the Web page come alive with the help of a few lines of VBScript.

USING THE COMMAND BUTTON CONTROL EVENTS

Your next objective is to manipulate the properties of the Text Box control with only a click of the mouse on the command button. When the user clicks `cmd1`, the Text Box displays the phrase `Thank You!`, and the background changes color.

Follow these steps to modify your application:

1. Click Tools, Script Wizard to begin. The Script Wizard will open, allowing you to modify properties through VBScript code.
2. Click the plus sign next to `cmd1` to view the available events. As you can see in Figure 12.4, there are many events that can be triggered by the Command Button Control.

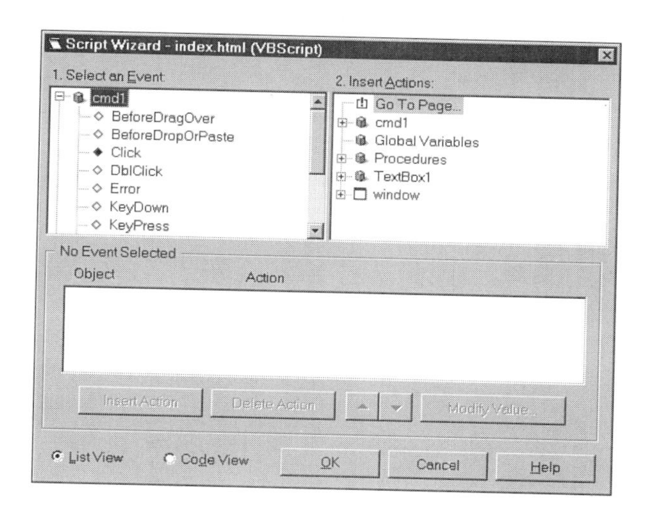

FIGURE 12.4 There are numerous events for you to choose from when designing your application.

Since the end user is clicking the command button to see a result, highlight the `Click` event listed under the Event pane. All that's left is to choose an action for the mouse click.

In the Action pane, click the plus sign next to `TextBox1`. All of the available properties are listed below the control. Select the `Text` property and type **Thank You!** inside the text box. Click OK to record your changes.

You also want the background color to change when the user clicks the button. This is as easy as adding a secondary action below your first. Follow these steps carefully to activate your controls further:

1. Select the `Click` event.
2. Double-click `BackColor` and choose a light color of your liking. Click OK.

Click OK once again to save your code. Save your new file as an HTML file and test it in a Web browser by browsing for it on your hard drive. Figure 12.5 illustrates what your page will look like within your browser.

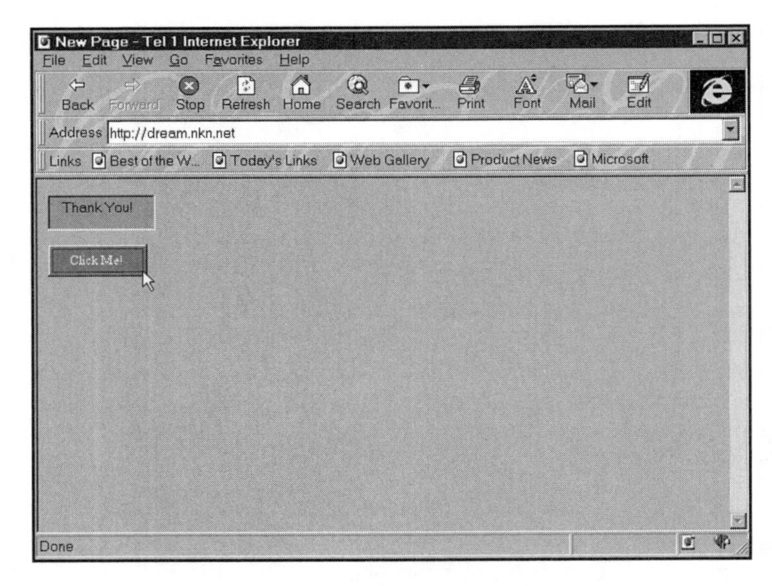

FIGURE 12.5 The most basic of ActiveX Control designs can lead to advanced uses later on down the road.

Click the command button called `Click Me!` to see the results of your work.

Though this is a very simple exercise, it proves a point about the ActiveX Control Pad—it takes very little effort to make a difference on a Web page. There are over 30 different actions that could have been performed by the Text Box Control when the Command Button was clicked. With a number of variations in each action, your application is one of millions of combinations that can be put to work.

Your final code looks like the following listing, with the proper order between scripting and object placement:

```
<HTML>
<HEAD>
<TITLE>New Page</TITLE>
</HEAD>
<BODY>
    <OBJECT ID="TextBox1" WIDTH=104
➥HEIGHT=35
     CLASSID="CLSID:8BD21D10-EC42-11CE-
➥9E0D-00AA006002F3">
        <PARAM NAME="VariousPropertyBits"
➥VALUE="746604571">
        <PARAM NAME="Size"
➥VALUE="2752;917">
        <PARAM NAME="FontCharSet"
➥VALUE="0">
        <PARAM NAME="FontPitchAndFamily"
➥VALUE="2">
    </OBJECT>
<P>
    <SCRIPT LANGUAGE="VBScript">
<!--
Sub cmd1_Click()
TextBox1.Text = "Thank You!"
TextBox1.BackColor = &H00FF8080
end sub
-->
```

```
    </SCRIPT>
    <OBJECT ID="cmd1" WIDTH=96 HEIGHT=32
     CLASSID="CLSID:D7053240-CE69-11CD-
➥A777-00DD01143C57">
<PARAM NAME="Caption" VALUE="Click Me!">
        <PARAM NAME="Size"
➥VALUE="2540;847">
        <PARAM NAME="FontName"
➥VALUE="Times New Roman">
        <PARAM NAME="FontHeight"
➥VALUE="200">
        <PARAM NAME="FontCharSet"
➥VALUE="0">
        <PARAM NAME="FontPitchAndFamily"
➥VALUE="2">
        <PARAM NAME="ParagraphAlign"
➥VALUE="3">
    </OBJECT>
</BODY>
</HTML>
```

The properties that you manipulated can easily be modified to change the background of the Text Box Control to a different color, the font a different size, and so on. With the addition of the Script Wizard, customizing a Web page with ActiveX controls is as easy as pointing and clicking.

In this lesson, you learned how to add a Command Button Control to a Web page to trigger certain effects. In the next lesson, you learn to use the Label Control to display text in a variety of colorful ways.

Using the Label Control

In this lesson, you learn how to use the Label Control to create interesting effects with text and manipulate the text through events.

Using the Label Control to Manipulate the Appearance of Text

Since the birth of HTML in 1993, Web authors have been limited to what they can do with text. Of course, you can format the text to take on different size, font, and color appearances, but actually controlling text on a path, or changing the display of the text at run-time, has only become possible with the help of ActiveX Controls.

As long as it is installed on the user's machine, the Label Control has the ability to display a line of text in any font, and the user can change it through quite a few built-in events. This is useful when you want to create a text-based animation or animated button without incorporating graphics.

To begin using the Label Control, follow these steps:

1. Create a new page in the ActiveX Control Pad.
2. Choose Edit, Insert ActiveX Control. Choose the Microsoft IE 30 Label Control from the Insert ActiveX Control list. Click OK to insert the control.

I don't have the IE30 Label Control! If you do not see Microsoft IE 30 Label Control listed in the Insert ActiveX Control dialog box, you might have it installed under the name of "Microsoft Forms 2.0 Label." These two controls function exactly the same way and share the same properties and events. If you do not have either of the controls, you will need to download one from **http://www.microsoft.com/activex/gallery/**.

Right now, the Label control that you have inserted has little function, but changing the many properties of the object remedies this situation.

USING THE LABEL CONTROL PROPERTIES

The Label Control has many properties to customize the display of the text. The following is a brief summary of the more useful properties:

- `Alignment` There are nine choices for the alignment of the text within the Label display cell. The options are:

  0—Left/Top alignment
  1—Center/Top alignment
  2—Right/Top alignment
  3—Left/Centered
  4—Centered
  5—Right/Centered
  6—Left/Bottom
  7—Centered/Bottom
  8—Right/Bottom

- `Back Style` This property has two choices, Transparent and Opaque. When set to transparent, the background color property will be overwritten with the settings of the background of your Web page.

- `Caption` Controls the physical text that will be displayed in the label.
- `Fill Style` Controls whether the Label will be a filled font or just display the outline of each letter.
- `Font Name` Controls the display appearance of the font. It is a good idea to stick with a font that most people will have installed on their machine, such as Arial or Courier.
- `Mode` Controls the mode in which the text will be rendered. The four choices are as follows:

  0—`Normal` This is set to keep the text on a straight path.
  1—`Simple rotation` Allows the text to be rotated at an angle.
  2—`User Defined No Rotation` Allows the end user to control the text's appearance without rotation abilities.
  3—`User Defined Rotation` Allows the end user to control the text's appearance with the ability to rotate the image.

Now that a few properties have been laid out, follow these steps to change the appearance of your Label control:

1. Highlight the `Alignment` property and click the drop-down list. Choose Centered and click Apply. This displays the text centered completely within the Label control.
2. Adjust the `Caption` property to say Label Control. Click Apply to save your changes.
3. Change the `Font Size` property by highlighting the property name and changing the value to 20. This makes the text much larger and easier to read.
4. Change the `ID` property to Label1. Click Apply to save your changes.

5. Change the `HEIGHT` and `WIDTH` properties to 200. This will create a cell that is 200 pixels square to contain your text.
6. Save your HTML page and view it with Internet Explorer to see the results of your work. Figure 13.1 illustrates how the page will look within your browser.

I can't read the Label Control! You may need to resize the Label control to read the contents of the Caption property. Do this by resizing the control with the mouse or by changing the Height and Width properties of the control in the Property Editor.

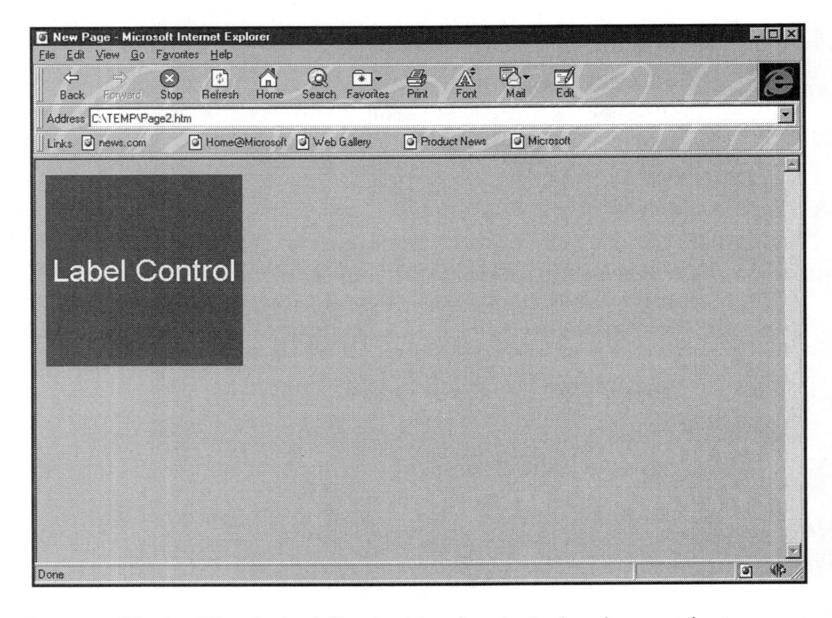

FIGURE 13.1 The Label Control is simple to implement but can take on any appearance that you want.

So far, your HTML code contains the following elements:

```
<HTML>
<HEAD>
<TITLE>New Page</TITLE>
</HEAD>
<BODY>
<OBJECT
         ID="label1"
         CLASSID="clsid:99B42120-6EC711CF-
➥A6C7-00AA00A47DD2"
            TYPE="application/x-oleobject"
         WIDTH=200
         HEIGHT=200
         VSPACE=0
         ALIGN=left
>
     <PARAM NAME="Angle" VALUE="0">
     <PARAM NAME="Alignment" VALUE="4" >
     <PARAM NAME="BackStyle" VALUE="1" >
     <PARAM NAME="BackColor" VALUE=
➥"#0000ff" >
     <PARAM NAME="Caption" VALUE="Label
➥Control">
     <PARAM NAME="FontName" VALUE="Arial">
     <PARAM NAME="FontSize" VALUE="24">
     <PARAM NAME="ForeColor" VALUE=
➥"#F0f000" >
     <PARAM NAME="FontBold" VALUE="0" >
</OBJECT>
</BODY>
</HTML>
```

Now that your Control appears as designed, you can begin to manipulate the Label through built-in events.

Hexadecimal Color Codes You will notice that the ForeColor and BackColor properties of the Label Control are different from the default settings. These values are actually hexadecimal color codes that will change the color of these two properties. Each hexadecimal value must be preceded with a # character in order to display correctly. For a handy hexadecimal reference chart, point your browser to **http://www.prgone.com/colors/**. Experiment with all of the color values of controls as you insert them to make your page stand out from others that use default color schemes.

USING THE LABEL CONTROL EVENTS

The Label Control contains six basic events, five of which are controlled exclusively with the mouse. Figure 13.2 shows all of the Label events available in the Script Wizard. The Label events are as follows:

- `MouseUp` Activated when the end user releases his or her mouse button while the cursor is focused on the Label.
- `MouseDown` Happens when the end user holds down the mouse button on the Label.
- `MouseMove` Activated when the user moves the mouse cursor across the Label cell.
- `Click` Enabled when the user clicks within the Label cell.
- `DblClick` Enabled when the user double-clicks within the Label cell.
- `OnChange` Activated when any of the Label's properties are changed. This is generally done through scripting languages.

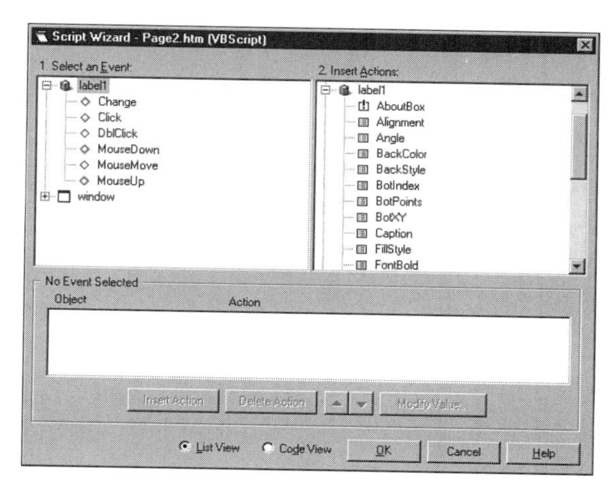

FIGURE 13.2 All of the Label Control's events can be accessed and manipulated through the Script Wizard.

My page appears blank! You have found a bug with the Label Control. If your Label page does not display correctly after adding script to your HTML, you will have to do a slight work around to get it to work. Try saving your HTML file with a different filename and loading it into your browser. Internet Explorer has some inconsistencies when it comes to storing ActiveX controls in the Cache directory and does not display pages correctly sometimes. Renaming the file should remedy the situation.

Now that the events are defined, you can change any properties of the window or Label Control with the Script Wizard. Simply highlight the event you wish to use, double-click the Action, and enter the change. All of the scripting code will be inserted into the HTML for you.

Follow these steps to cause your Label to respond to a user's mouse click:

1. Click Tools, Script Wizard to begin scripting.
2. Click the plus sign next to Label1 to expand the Events available to the control.
3. Select Click by clicking on the Event.
4. In the Action Pane, expand the actions available to the window. Also expand the list of document properties by clicking the plus.
5. Double-click on `bgColor` and type **Black** in the window. Click OK.
6. Click OK once more to close the Script Wizard.

The following code is inserted above the Label control in your HTML document:

```
<SCRIPT LANGUAGE="VBScript">
<!--
Sub Label1_Click()
window.document.bgColor = "Black"
end sub
-->
    </SCRIPT>
```

When you view the HTML page in Internet Explorer, clicking the Label control will turn the background of the Web page black. Experiment by using the Label control to trigger other browser actions such as opening a new Web page or changing the color of text that is displayed on the screen.

In this lesson, you learned how to use the Label control to create interesting blocks of text that can be manipulated through events. In the next lesson, you use the Timer Control to automate the activation of other ActiveX controls.

Using the Timer Control

In this lesson, you learn how to use the Timer Control to activate other controls at different time intervals.

Using the Timer to Control Events

By now, you are becoming accustomed to incorporating ActiveX Controls into your HTML documents. As your skills evolve, however, you will eventually want to designate when your controls go into effect, periodically change a control's properties, and invoke instances of timed responses to user events. The Timer Control included with Internet Explorer 3.0 enables you to adjust the timing of all your events through an extra control on your page and some VBScript.

The Timer Control is completely invisible at runtime. Its only purpose is to put your events on a time-based scale, making your controls active when you choose. In this example, you create two controls in a new HTML page: a Label Control that is essentially a simple text message, and a Timer Control that controls when the Label's properties are changed.

Begin by creating a blank page in the ActiveX Control Pad and follow these steps:

1. Click Edit, Insert ActiveX Control. Choose Microsoft IE 30 label from the Insert ActiveX Control list.
2. Change the `ID` to `label` in the Properties window.
3. Adjust the `Font Size` to 16 by highlighting the property name and typing in a new value at the top.

4. Change the `Caption` property to Timer Test. Click Apply to save your changes.
5. Close both the Properties window and the Edit ActiveX Control window.

Right now your new Web page is functional, but the Label Control does nothing but sit on the page and display the words "Timer Test." Once you add the timer, however, your control can change as the viewer reads the page. Figure 14.1 demonstrates how your page looks before you add a second control.

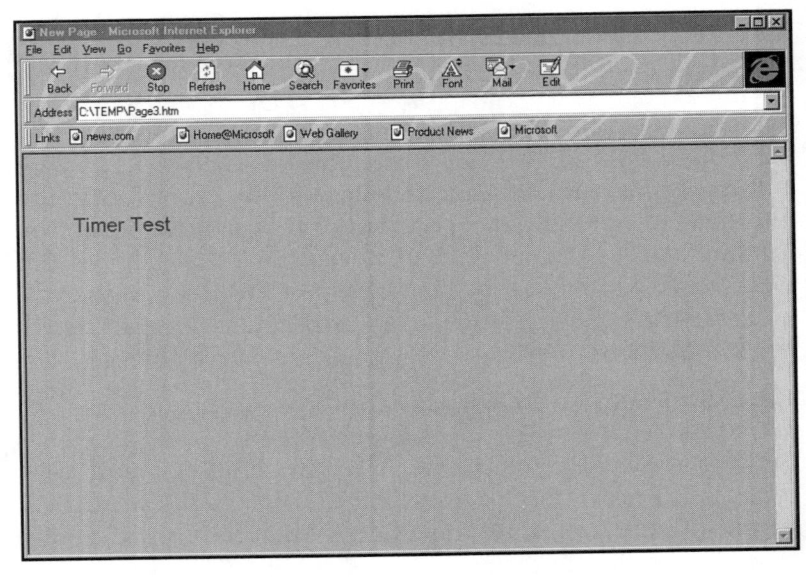

FIGURE 14.1 Quite often, ActiveX Controls need to be taken a step further toward activation by adding multiple controls to your Web page.

Go ahead and add the Timer Control to your page now by using the following steps. After the control is inserted, explore the Timer Control properties to see how they can work best for you.

1. Click Edit, Insert ActiveX Control. Choose the Microsoft IE 30 Timer Control from the Insert ActiveX Control window and click OK.

2. Close the Properties window and the Edit ActiveX Control window for now.

The next section explores the limited properties of the Timer Control and how you can begin manipulating objects with timed responses.

I can't read the text! You may need to resize your Label Control to read all of the text contained within the `Caption` property. To do this, drag the edges of the control until you can see all of the message or adjust the `Height` and `Width` properties of the control within the Property Editor.

USING THE TIMER CONTROL PROPERTIES

The Timer Control has only two real properties that affect its operation. These properties are `Enabled` and `Interval`.

The `Enabled` property can be set to either `True` or `False`. Setting this control property to `True` makes the control active as soon as it is loaded. A setting of `False` makes the control inoperable until it's triggered by an ActiveX Control such as the Command Button Control or another Timer Control.

The `Interval` property controls the amount of time that passes between each Timer controlled event. The scale of the `Interval` property is recorded in milliseconds. Hence, a setting of 1000 causes the Timer to wait one full second between events. A setting of 250 causes the Timer to activate every quarter of a second. A negative value for the `Interval` property results in disabling the Timer, even if you have the `Enabled` property set to `True`.

Now it's time to change the properties of your Timer Control; use the following steps:

1. Click the Edit ActiveX Control icon next to the Timer Control to open the Edit ActiveX Control window and Properties window.

2. Change the `Interval` property to 500. This causes your timer to use an interval of half a second between events.

3. Change the `ID` of the Timer to `Timer1`. This is not required in all of your projects but is used for the sake of simplicity in this HTML page.

4. Close the Properties window and the Edit ActiveX Control window to record your changes.

So far, your code should look something like the following:

```
<HTML>
<HEAD>
<TITLE>New Page</TITLE>
</HEAD>
<BODY>
<OBJECT
        ID=label
        CLASSID="clsid:99B42120-6EC711CF-
➥A6C7-00AA00A47DD2"
        WIDTH=120
        HEIGHT=120
        ALIGN=left
        HSPACE=30
        VSPACE=0
>
    <PARAM NAME="Alignment" VALUE="4">
    <PARAM NAME="BackStyle" VALUE="0">
    <PARAM NAME="Caption" VALUE="Timer
➥Test">
    <PARAM NAME="ForeColor" VALUE=
➥"#000000">
    <PARAM NAME="FontName" VALUE="Arial">
    <PARAM NAME="FontSize" VALUE="16">
</OBJECT>
<OBJECT ID="Timer1" WIDTH=39 HEIGHT=39
CLASSID="CLSID:59CCB4A0-727D-11CF-AC36-
➥00AA00A47DD2">
```

```
    <PARAM NAME="_ExtentX" VALUE="1005">
    <PARAM NAME="_ExtentY" VALUE="1005">
    <PARAM NAME="Interval" VALUE="500">
</OBJECT>
</BODY>
</HTML>
```

Even though the Timer Control is included, and configured into your HTML page, when you save and reload it in your Web browser it cannot function correctly yet. By adding a couple of lines of VBScript, however, your label activates before your user's eyes.

USING VBSCRIPT WITH THE TIMER CONTROL

In this example, you rotate the Label Control five degrees every half second with the Timer Control and VBScript. Use the following steps:

1. Insert the following VBScript code beneath the `</OBJECT>` tag of the second control:

```
<!----
<SCRIPT LANGUAGE="VBScript">
Sub Timer1_Timer
     Label.Angle = (Label.Angle - 5) mod
360
End Sub
</SCRIPT>
---->
```

My text is getting cut off! You might need to resize the `Height` and `Width` properties so that the rotating text appears completely within the label. Use the Property Editor or add your parameters by hand to change the size of the Label Control.

2. Save your HTML file and reload it in your Web browser. Your page should look like Figure 14.2.

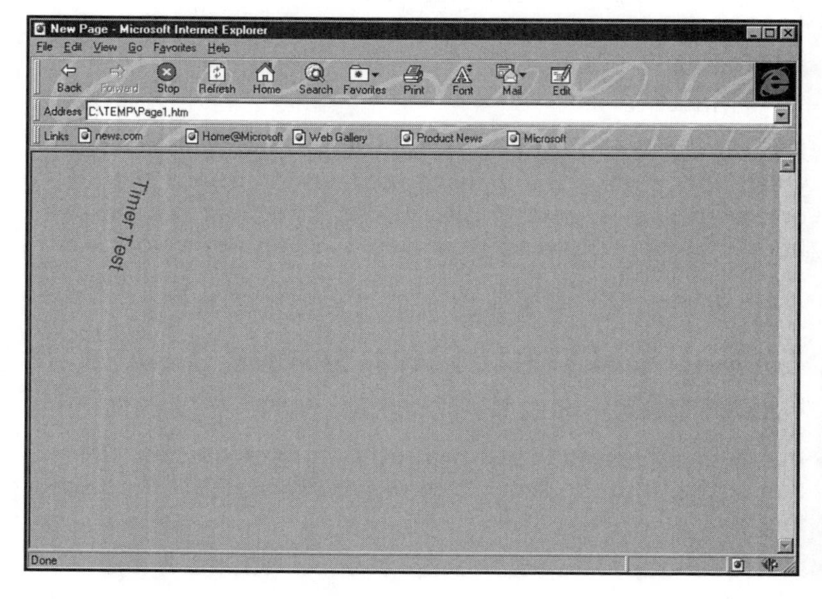

FIGURE 14. 2 Though rotating the Label is a simple process, it can lead to very big possibilities.

In this VBScript example, the Timer Control changes the `.angle` property of the Label to move five degrees clockwise at every interval in the range of a complete circle. As the Label rotates, it keeps spinning on its center axis.

You can modify any of the Label's properties and change the control's look or function with ease through VBScript. A Command Button Control could have also been placed on the page to control the movement of the Label like a light switch.

In this chapter, you learned how to use the Timer Control to manipulate another ActiveX Control at a predefined interval. In the next lesson, you learn to use the Preloader Control to download files to the viewers cache directory while browsers view another page.

USING THE PRELOADER CONTROL

In this lesson, you learn how to decrease your Web site viewer's download time by using the Preloader Control.

USING THE PRELOADER CONTROL TO DECREASE DOWNLOAD TIME

One of the most frustrating aspects of viewing pages on the World Wide Web is the amount of time that it takes to download pages. But what if you could download another page to your viewer as he or she views the first? That would be a fantastic achievement and is possible through the use of the Preloader ActiveX Control that is built into Internet Explorer 3.0.

The Preloader Control is simple to use because of the nature of its functionality. Its sole purpose is to preload the contents of a target URL or file to the browser's cache so that the document can be opened quickly.

I don't have IE30 Preloader Control! You might have the Preloader Control registered on your system under the name Preloader Object. This control functions exactly the same as the IE30 Preloader Control, and all of the events and properties are identical. If you do not have either of the controls, download a copy from **http://www.microsoft.com/activex/gallery/**.

To incorporate the Preloader Control into your Web pages, use the following steps:

1. Open the Web page you want to edit in the ActiveX Control Pad.
2. Click Edit, Insert ActiveX Control.
3. Choose Microsoft IE 30 Preloader Control from the Insert ActiveX Control menu and click OK.

The Preloader Control is inserted into your document and the properties are ready to be edited with the Property Editor.

USING THE PRELOADER CONTROL PROPERTIES

There are only two properties of the Preloader Control that you can modify. These properties are the `URL` and `Enable` parameters.

The `URL` property is the file or Web page that is downloaded into the cache when the control is enabled. The `Enable` property automatically starts the preloading process when set to a value of 1. When set to 0, the Timer Control can easily trigger when the preload takes place.

For now, set these two properties by following these steps:

1. Select the `URL` property in the Property Editor and type **http://www.usatoday.com/index.html** into the empty text box. Click Apply.
2. Select the `Enable` property and change the value to 1 so that the page loads right away (see Figure 15.1).

Your code looks like the following:

```
<HTML>
<HEAD>
<TITLE>New Page</TITLE>
</HEAD>
<BODY>
        <OBJECT ID="PreLoader1" WIDTH=0
➥HEIGHT=0
 CLASSID="CLSID:16E349E0-702C-11CF-A3A9-
➥00A0C9034920">
```

```
    <PARAM NAME="_ExtentX" VALUE="0">
    <PARAM NAME="_ExtentY" VALUE="0">
    <PARAM NAME="URL" VALUE="http://
➥www.usatoday.com/index.html">
    <PARAM NAME="enable" VALUE="1">
</OBJECT>
</BODY>
</HTML>
```

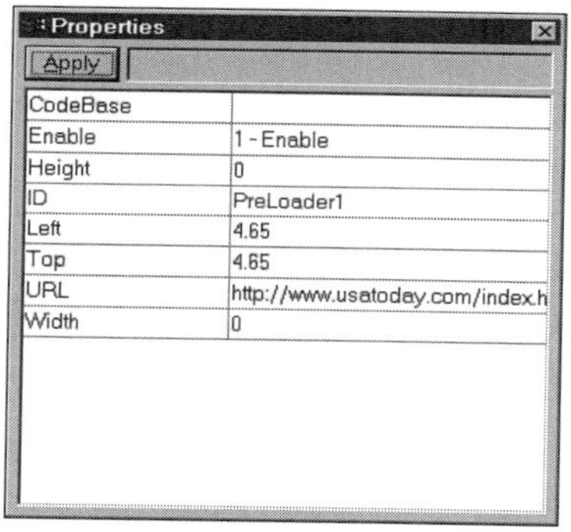

Properties

Apply

CodeBase	
Enable	1 - Enable
Height	0
ID	PreLoader1
Left	4.65
Top	4.65
URL	http://www.usatoday.com/index.h
Width	0

FIGURE 15.1 Though there are few properties to modify within the Preloader Control, the effects are incredible.

USING THE PRELOADER CONTROL EVENTS

There are only two events that the Preloader Control has attached to it: `Complete` and `Error`.

- `Complete` Launches once the download process is completed.
- `Error` Launches when the Preloader Control fails to function as intended.

Though there are only two events, you can use both in the same file for great debugging techniques. The following VBScript code example will send either a confirmation message denoting a successful preload or an error message, depending (see Figure 15.2) on the outcome of the event:

```
<SCRIPT LANGUAGE="VBScript">
<!--
Sub PreLoader1_Complete()
     alert "The URL " & PreLoader1.URL &
➥"has been preloaded to " &
PreLoader1.CacheFile
End Sub
Sub PreLoader1_Error()
     alert "Whoops, your code is goofed
➥up!"
End Sub
-->
    </SCRIPT>
```

> **TIP**
>
> **Entering Scripts by Hand** When you have a script that needs to be inserted into a Web page, it is often much quicker to do so by hand rather than entering it into the Script Wizard. It is good practice to place all of your scripts below any ActiveX control so that the page is displayed as intended.

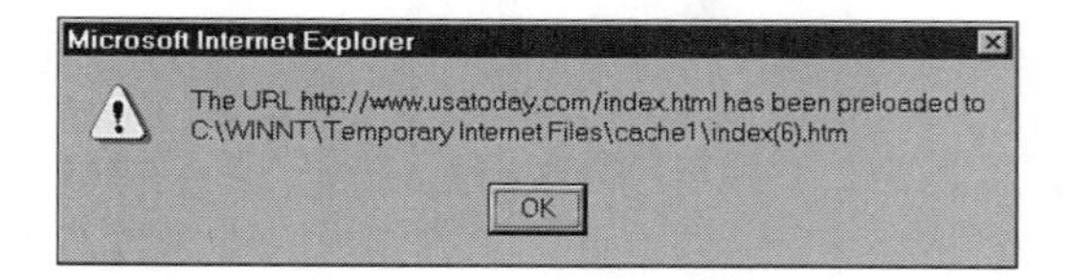

Figure 15.2 Effective messaging helps you and your Web site visitors get the most out of your controls.

> **TIP**
>
> **Use Message Boxes Effectively** Though message boxes can be used to notify the user when something has gone awry or a process is completed, using too many can be overkill. Try to limit the use of message boxes by perfecting your scripts and putting more information within the body of the HTML page itself.

Using the Preloader Control Effectively

As you gain an understanding of how the Preloader Control is used, your mind will begin to wander and soon you will be thinking of thousands of uses for the control. Be warned, however, overusing this control is easy.

You should not use the Preloader Control to load all of the pages in your Web site. This is a waste of Internet bandwidth and can be useless unless you know that the viewer will proceed on to the next page. The control can be used effectively, however, to preload your main Web page from an introductory page. This is very useful when your introductory page contains a small graphic or message to gain the reader's attention and then leads into your main page. The main page downloads as the user views the message on the first page.

Perhaps you have a portion of your Web site that contains long lists of products or many small graphics for an online catalog. The Preloader Control is used effectively in this situation by loading the list or graphics while the user reads about how to order and how items are organized.

The Preloader Control is very powerful in the fact that it can take control of your visitor's browser and download what you want it to. Many users will take offense at this though. All of the files that you preload to the browser are stored in the cache on the hard drive. For users with limited hard drive space, this can eat up valuable disk resources and frustrate the user by forcing them to delete files from his or her hard drive. While this scenario might seem far-fetched, many Internet users are using older computers where free hard drive space is still a very big issue.

Remember that the Preloader Control can be used multiple times on a Web page to download various files in the background. With this in mind, do not attempt to download an entire Web page with many graphics to a user's browser. If the user does not end up visiting the next page, you have wasted not only the user's resources but valuable Web-server resources as well.

In this chapter, you learned how to use the Preloader Control to speed up Web page downloading. In the next lesson, you learn to use the Marquee Control to scroll one Web page within another.

Using the Marquee Control

In this lesson, will learn how to incorporate moving text into your Web site through the use of the Marquee ActiveX Control.

Using the Marquee Control to Animate Static Text

Web pages are now in a transition of moving from static content to active pages. This is evident with the popularity of ActiveX Controls and the release of the ActiveX Control Pad. Microsoft released a special HTML tag, called `<MARQUEE>`, in the release of Internet Explorer 2.0 that allowed lines of text to scroll across a Web page as though it were an animated GIF or Java applet. Built into Internet Explorer 3.0 however, is an ActiveX Control that allows entire Web pages to be "animated" across a Web page.

What is an active Web page? An active Web page does more than display text and graphics. Through the use of ActiveX controls and scripting languages, you can enrich your Web site viewer's experience by animating your content and providing user interaction with buttons and menus. This will give the user an environment of interactivity, instead of a one-sided, flat Web page.

Why would you use such a feature? A marquee that scrolls product offerings across the top of your company's Web page will give readers a hint of what your company is all about before they really get into your Web site. The Marquee control can be used anywhere that you want to display information in a manner that is guaranteed to gain attention and can be updated quickly.

The Marquee control relies on a referenced Web site address that contains the information intended for display. You can use this to display a page from a Web site other than your own, or to simply display a Web page containing a mix of graphics and text to provide a message or advertisement.

To see the Marquee control in action, point your browser to **http://microsoft.saltmine.com/activexisv/msctls/ie/marquee.htm**. This Web page not only illustrates how the Marquee control can be used, but also how it can be changed through Command Button events. By clicking the Command Buttons you can alter the speed of the Marquee and then restore it to the normal settings. Click View, Source to get an idea of how this effect is achieved. Figure 16.1 illustrates the Marquee control in action.

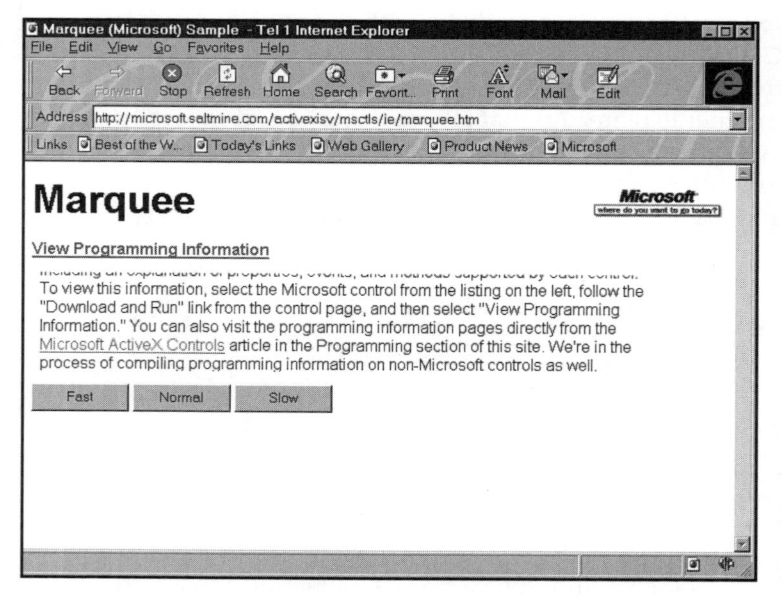

FIGURE 16. 1 Microsoft's use of the Marquee ActiveX control is one of many uses that you can incorporate into your Web pages.

To insert the Marquee control into your own Web site, follow these steps:

1. Open the ActiveX Control Pad to a blank page.
2. Click Edit, Insert ActiveX Control.
3. Choose Microsoft IE 30 Marquee Control to insert the element into your Web page.

The Marquee is another control like the Popup Menu Control that is not actually displayed in your Web page itself, and therefore it does not matter how the control itself is sized. The Control will eventually utilize a target URL that will be used in your page.

The Marquee loads so slowly! If you feel that your Marquee control is loading into the Web page too slowly, you might try setting the `DrawImmediately` property to zero. Though the control will not be displayed as soon as the page loads, the marquee will scroll smoothly after being downloaded completely.

USING THE MARQUEE CONTROL PROPERTIES

After your control is inserted into your Web page, there are a handful of important properties for you to modify to ensure that your Marquee element will display correctly.

The most important property is that of the `SzURL`. This specifies the target URL that will be displayed in your Marquee. This parameter statement must follow the outlined style:

```
<PARAM NAME="szURL" VALUE="http://
➥location.domain.com/file.html">
```

The `DrawImmediately` parameter specifies whether the URL should be displayed as it is downloaded to the browser or after it has been downloaded to the cache. The default value is 1 (`true`) which will paint the URL as it is received. The following syntax must be used when using this property:

```
<PARAM NAME="DrawImmediately" VALUE="1">
```

`ScrollPixelsX` is responsible for the amount of the overall URL that is displayed horizontally in the time stated in `ScrollDelay`. The unit of measurement is in pixels, with the default being 75 pixels displayed every second. A negative value will cause the Marquee to move to the left. Use this parameter in the following way:

```
<PARAM NAME="ScrollPixelsX" VALUE="75"> or
<PARAM NAME="ScrollPixelsX" VALUE="-75">
```

`ScrollPixelsY` is the opposite of `ScrollPixelsX`. This value is responsible for the vertical movement of the Marquee. A negative `VALUE` within this property will cause the Marquee to scroll down instead of up. The `ScrollPixelsY` parameter is used in this fashion:

```
<PARAM NAME="ScrollPixelsY" VALUE="75"> or
<PARAM NAME="ScrollPixelsY" VALUE="-75">
```

The `Zoom` property allows you to size the URL currently being displayed in the Marquee. A value of 100 will cause the URL to be displayed in its normal size, and a value of 50 will cause the URL to be displayed at half of its original size. The `VALUE` must be a positive integer between 1 and 100. The syntax for the `Zoom` parameter is as follows:

```
<PARAM NAME="Zoom" VALUE="100">
```

`WidthOfPage` is responsible for the overall width that the Marquee will take up in your Web page. The default value is 640, which will allow the average viewer to see the entire width of the Marquee that is being displayed. Follow this syntax for the `WidthOfPage` property:

```
<PARAM NAME="WidthOfPage" VALUE="640">
```

Inserting the following code into a blank HTML document will demonstrate the power of the Marquee Control (see Figure 16.2):

```
<HTML>
<HEAD>
<TITLE>New Page</TITLE>
</HEAD>
<BODY>
<OBJECT
    ID="Marquee1"
      CLASSID="CLSID:1A4DA620-6217-11CF-
➥BE62-0080C72EDD2D"
     TYPE="application/x-oleobject"
     WIDTH=100%
     HEIGHT=100>
     <PARAM NAME="szURL" VALUE="http://
➥www.usatoday.com/index.html">
     <PARAM NAME="ScrollPixelsX"
➥VALUE="0">
     <PARAM NAME="DrawImmediately"
➥VALUE="0">
     <PARAM NAME="Zoom" VALUE="100">
     <PARAM NAME="WidthOfPage"
➥VALUE="640">
          <PARAM NAME="ScrollPixelsY"
➥VALUE="-5">
          <PARAM NAME="ScrollDelay"
➥VALUE="100">
          <PARAM NAME="Whitespace"
➥VALUE="0">
</OBJECT>
<P>
<h2>USA Today Online</h2>
</BODY>
</HTML>
```

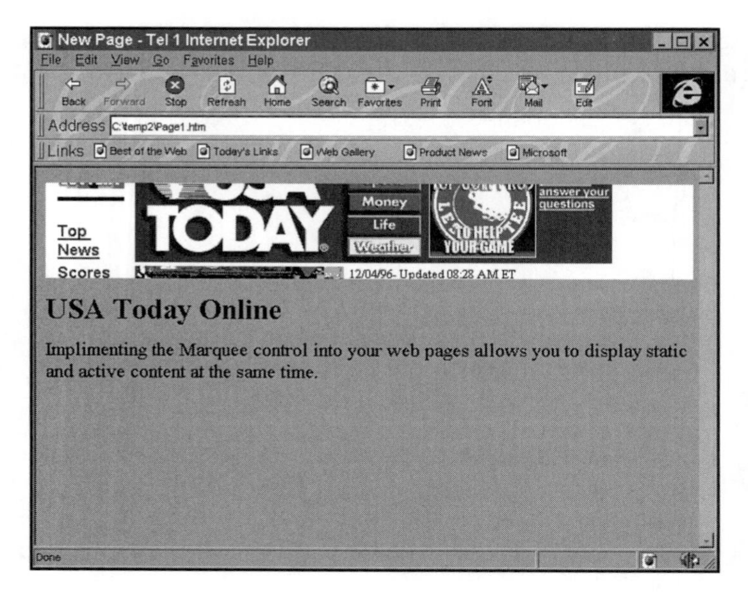

FIGURE 16. 2 Using the Marquee control within your Web pages is an easy way to display two types of content—static and active.

USING THE MARQUEE CONTROL EVENTS

The Marquee Control has only five events that are possible to invoke. All five can be accessed from the Script Wizard as in previous lessons. The five events are:

`OnLMouseClick` Happens when the user clicks the mouse button anywhere within the Marquee control.

`OnStartOfImage` Occurs just before the Marquee image begins to scroll.

`OnEndOfImage` This occurs just as the Marquee image ends its scrolling process.

`OnBounce` Only occurs when the value Bounce is enabled within the `ScrollStyle` property. The event occurs as soon as the Marquee image "bounces" off of one side of the control.

`OnScroll` Occurs each time the Marquee image begins to scroll.

The majority of Web developers will simply use the `OnLMouseClick` event. This event can easily be used to trigger the Web browser to open the `szURL` target in the entire window. To add this functionality to the *USA Today* preview page, follow these steps:

1. Open the Script Wizard.
2. Select the `OnLMouseClick` event under the Marquee control.
3. In the action pane, choose `window.location.href`. The value should be entered as **http://www.usatoday.com/index.html**.

Your VBScript will look like the following code example:

```
<SCRIPT LANGUAGE="VBScript">
<!--
Sub Marquee1_OnLMouseClick()
window.location.href = "http://www.
➥usatoday.com/index.html"
end sub
-->
    </SCRIPT>
```

Now, if you reload the activated Web page and click the *USA Today* Marquee, the mouse click event will trigger the browser to display the full Web page.

The Marquee is doubling my download time! While using the Marquee in your Web page will increase download time, the content of the page will always load before the content of the Marquee. This allows your Web site visitor to navigate your Web page normally if they do not wish to wait until the Marquee fully downloads.

In this lesson, you learned how to incorporate the Marquee control into a Web page and manipulate the properties and events to change the overall look and function. In the next lesson, you will explore the possibilities of creating your own ActiveX Controls with the Visual Basic 5.0 Control Creation Edition.

Building Your Own ActiveX Controls

In this lesson, you learn how to create your own ActiveX control from scratch with the help of Visual Basic Control Creation Edition.

Creating Custom ActiveX Controls

By now, you have learned quite a bit about ActiveX controls and activating your Web site with the ActiveX Control Pad. Earlier lessons have introduced six ActiveX Controls, contained within Internet Explorer and the ActiveX Control Pad, that you can use right away. But what if the default controls don't fit your needs? You're in luck. With the help of Visual Basic 5.0 Control Creation Edition (VB CCE), you can create ActiveX controls from the ground up and start using them right away.

The VB CCE is available free of charge at Microsoft's Web site. Once installed, you can create ActiveX controls from the exact same interface that VB 5 and the rest of the Microsoft developer applications share. If you're new to Visual Basic, then the VB CCE is a great place to learn the basics of the language.

You might be wondering why you would want to create custom ActiveX controls. Though you may be able to create an interactive Web page with existing controls, you will probably find that it's easier to create your own custom components than manipulating someone else's controls. Another great advantage of using the VB CCE for ActiveX development is the fact that you can use multiple controls during design time and compile them into one single .Ocx file to use in your Web pages. Once you compile an .Ocx, your control is automatically registered into your system and a CLASSID is assigned.

What's an .Ocx? An .Ocx file is the core of an ActiveX control. It is actually made up of lines of programming code that has been compiled, or structured, into a functional file. When you encounter an ActiveX control that is new to your system, the .Ocx file is entered in the Windows Registry where important system settings are retained. After the .Ocx is installed, the control is made available to programs such as the ActiveX Control Pad, allowing you to insert them into your own custom applications.

CLASSID CLASSID is the abbreviated term for a Class Identifier. The Class Identifier provides a unique identifier for installed ActiveX Controls. The CLASSID itself is a cryptic group of letters and numbers that can be utilized by multiple programs without having to download the same component every time.

Downloading and Installing Visual Basic Control Creation Edition

The VB CCE is freely downloadable from Microsoft's Web site at **http://www.microsoft.com/vbasic/controls/download/default.htm**. The base installation itself is over 7M in size and takes roughly 45 minutes to download on a 28.8Kbps modem. Once you have acquired the initial compressed file, download the additional help files located at the same URL.

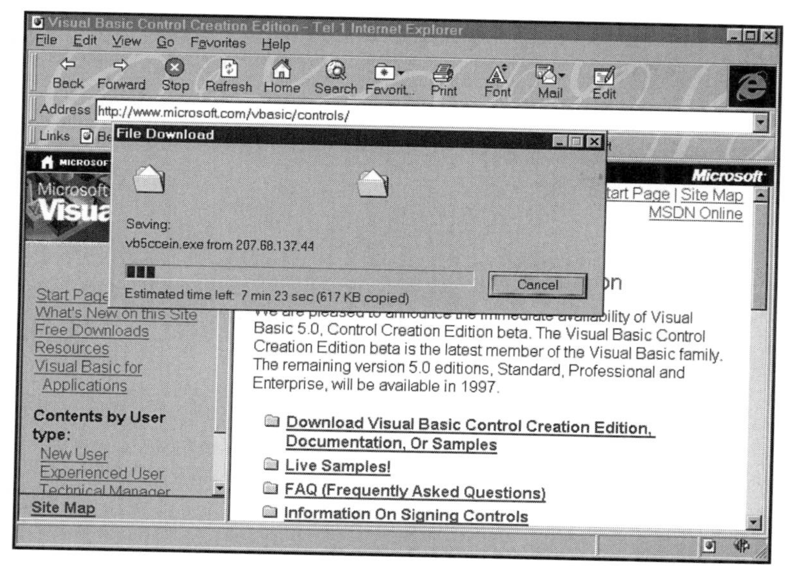

FIGURE 17.1 Downloading the VB CCE takes some time, but it's worth it.

To download the VB CCE, follow these steps:

1. Open **http://www.microsoft.com/vbasic/controls/download/default.htm** within your Web browser.
2. Click the `Registration Form` link to join Microsoft's Site Builder Network as a Guest. This is a free process that takes only a couple of minutes.
3. Return to the VB CCE download page after you have received your password from the Site Builder Network. Click `Guest Download` and enter your username and password in the appropriate fields. Click OK to go to the Guest Download page.
4. Click `Download Now` and choose Visual Basic 5.0 Control Creation Edition from the drop-down menu and click the `Go to Download` button.
5. Click the download location that is geographically closest to you.

After a few seconds, the file begins downloading to your computer. When prompted, choose Save to Disk and click OK. Find a directory to save the file to on your hard drive and click Save.

Once the file has completed downloading, you need to browse your hard drive and find the directory where you saved the file. Once you've located the file, double-click it to begin the installation process.

The installation process installs VB CCE onto your hard drive and creates the appropriate icons on the Start menu. Once completed, you can delete the file that you downloaded originally. You also need to reboot your computer before you can begin creating ActiveX Controls. To launch the VB CCE program, click Start (Ctrl+Esc), Programs, Microsoft Visual Basic, Visual Basic 5.0 Control Creation Edition.

USING THE VB CCE INTERFACE

Every time you open the CCE, you are presented with a choice of projects to build. Double-click the ActiveX Control icon to begin developing your own control.

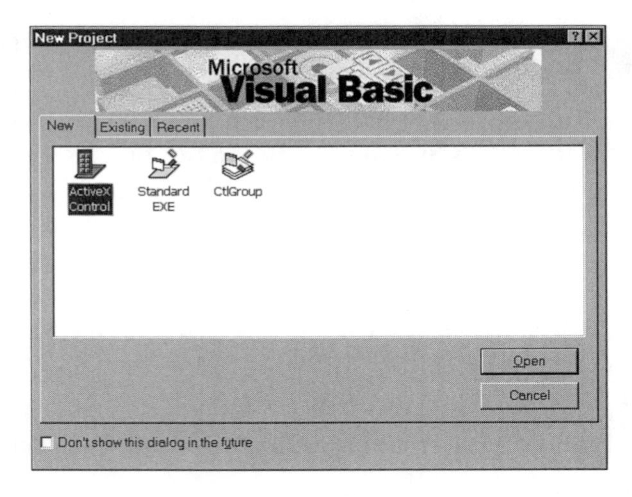

FIGURE 17.2 Choose the ActiveX Control icon from the window to begin your custom development.

By default, the CCE starts with the Project, Properties, and Form Layout windows open. A blank form is also created for you to begin working with. To access the Form toolbox, click View (Alt+V), Toolbox. The tools appear on the left side of your screen allowing you to begin designing your form immediately.

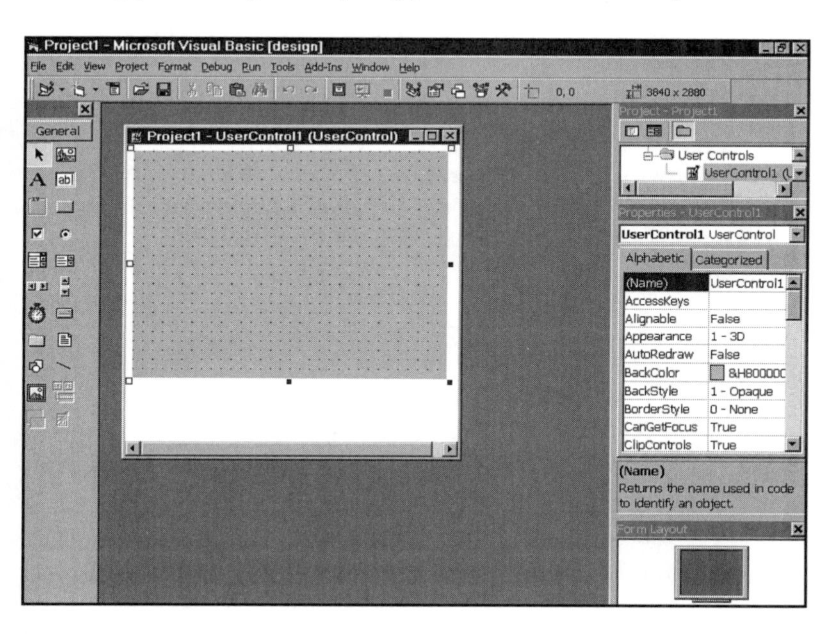

FIGURE 17.3 Opening all of the necessary windows puts all of your design elements within easy reach.

The Properties window operates much like the Object Editor in the ActiveX Control Pad. To change the property of an item, simply click in the field that you want to change and make the change within that box. All physical form and component changes are seen immediately.

The Form toolbox houses a default set of ActiveX controls for you to combine and use within your custom control. If you hold your mouse cursor over one control long enough, a box appears that identifies the name of the control. To use the control in your form, simply click the element that you want to use and draw it on the form. Some elements, such as the Timer, do not need to be sized and you should not worry about controlling how they appear on-screen. As you add controls onto your form, the properties window changes to reflect the currently selected control.

The Project window houses all of your modules and forms like the Script Wizard organizes procedures and global variables in the ActiveX Control Pad. The Project window acts as a container for your entire project, allowing you to edit any portion by double-clicking the item.

The Layout window is designed to give you an idea of how big your control will be on different monitors. The best rule of thumb is to keep all elements within the 640×480 resolution so that it looks proper on all monitors.

Reducing Screen Clutter When creating a new form you may want to clear the screen of any extra windows and toolbars so that you can view the application easier. To close the windows, simply click the X in the upper-right hand corner. If you wish to remove some of the toolbars, drag the toolbar from the top of the screen, using the mouse, and close it like you would a normal window. When you need these tools and windows again, click the View menu and click the appropriate choice.

Using Custom ActiveX Controls in Your Web Applications

After you build your ActiveX Control, you must compile it into an .Ocx file that is useable by the ActiveX Control Pad. To see how compiling an application works, use the following steps:

1. Click File, New Project, or Ctrl+N to create a blank form and project. A blank form will appear, ready for your ActiveX controls.

2. Click File, Save Project As, and rename your project by typing **mycontrol** into the text box.
3. Click File, Make mycontrol.ocx from the menu to compile your application into a functional resource.

As your application is being compiled, the .Ocx is issued a `CLASSID` and an entry is made in the Registry to register the control. Now that you have generated an .Ocx file, you can insert the control into the ActiveX Control Pad, using the following steps:

1. Open the ActiveX Control Pad to a blank page.
2. Click Edit, Insert ActiveX Control. The Insert ActiveX dialog box will appear, listing all of the installed controls that reside on your system.
3. Choose `Mycontrol` from the list. The empty form that is created by default in the VB CCE is inserted into your Web page.

Though this control offers no real functionality, it demonstrates how easy it is to use the VB CCE to author and compile an ActiveX Control from the ground up. As your programming skills increase, you will find interesting ways of combining and reusing ActiveX Controls in your Web site.

In this lesson, you learned how to install and use the Visual Basic Control Creation Edition to create your own ActiveX controls. In the next lesson you will find out where to obtain additional ActiveX controls and how they can be utilized in a Web page.

LESSON 18

Downloading Additional Controls

In this lesson, you learn where to download additional ActiveX controls and what new controls will do for your Web pages.

Downloading Additional Controls

In previous lessons you have seen how to include ActiveX controls in Web pages, change a control's properties with the Property Editor, and use VBScript to modify how a control is used. By now, you have probably looked through the list of ActiveX controls available to you in the Insert ActiveX Control dialog box and are now probably wondering how and where to acquire additional controls.

The best place to download additional controls is from the ActiveX Gallery in Microsoft's Site Builder Workshop Web site. The Gallery is located at **http://www.microsoft.com/activex/gallery/**. Here you will find the most comprehensive list of ActiveX controls available on the Internet today. The ActiveX Gallery is shown in Figure 18.1.

There are currently over 100 ActiveX controls available for downloading from the ActiveX Control Gallery. Each ActiveX control is listed in order by the company that created it, and a hyperlink is provided for each control to access more information and to download the component itself.

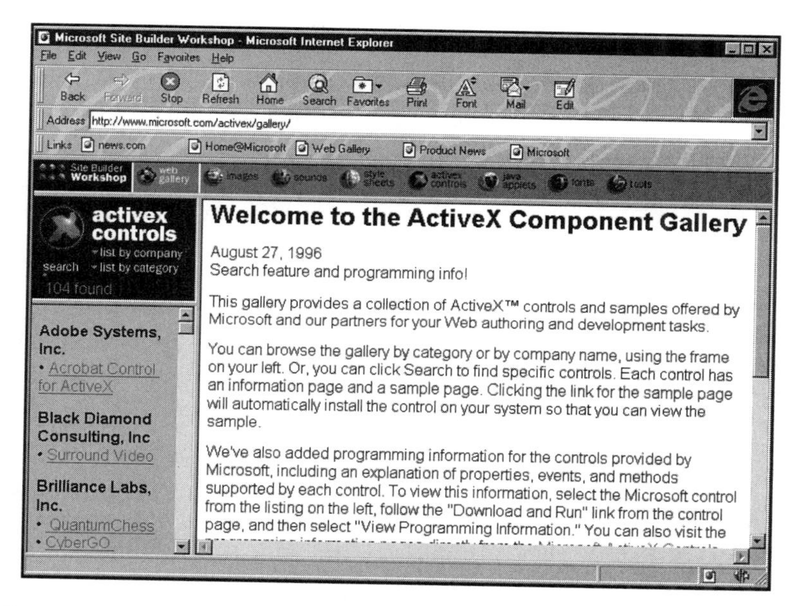

FIGURE 18.1 Microsoft's ActiveX Control Gallery is the best resource for obtaining additional ActiveX controls.

Follow these steps to download an additional control:

1. Click File, Open in Internet Explorer. The Open dialog box will appear. Type the address **http://www.microsoft.com/activex/gallery/** into the text box and click OK. The ActiveX Gallery will open, displaying a long list of available controls.

2. Scroll down the left frame window and click the hyperlink titled **Liquid Motion Player** under the Dimension X heading. General information about the control's function, and how to acquire further information, is listed on the new Web page that appears.

3. Click the link Download and run a working sample of this control. A new Web page will open and the control

will begin installing immediately. You will see a message appear in the status bar that says "Installing components" as the ActiveX controls are downloaded to your computer. The control is only 64K in size and should only take about one minute to download.

4. Click Yes when the Authenticode Security Technology window appears. This will allow the safe control to be downloaded fully.

Once the control is fully installed, a Liquid Motion animation will appear in place of the blank ActiveX control box, showing you that the control installed correctly and functions properly.

ActiveX Control Box You will encounter a Web page that references an ActiveX control that you do not have installed, an empty box with a colored diamond will appear in the page. This signifies that you are accessing a Web page with an ActiveX control that you do not have the capability to display in your browser. Most of the time you will be prompted by, or be provided with, a hyperlink to download the control. If not, the CODEBASE property has not been used effectively and you will have to get the control from the software company's Web page.

Some larger controls install much like other Windows programs with a separate installer program that is run as soon as the component is fully downloaded. If you encounter an ActiveX control that installs this way, you will need to close down any other programs that you currently have running before installing so the system files can be updated if they are out of date. You may also have to reboot your computer after the installation routine is complete.

Why do I have to reboot? If a system file is updated, you will not be able to use the new file until your system is rebooted. You can always choose not to reboot, but you will not be able to use the new ActiveX control until you do.

Once a control is downloaded and installed into your machine, it is immediately available for use with the ActiveX Control Pad. To check the availability of a control on your system, follow these steps:

1. Open the ActiveX Control Pad.
2. Choose Edit, Insert ActiveX Control. The Insert ActiveX Control dialog box will appear.
3. Scroll down the list until you see the control that you have just installed.

It's not there! Some controls are not meant to be inserted into one of your own HTML applications. Many controls are used only to access information, not supply it. Therefore, you will not be able to incorporate every ActiveX control that you download into a Web page.

ActiveX controls will vary in how much disk space they use on your system. Controls can range from only 10K in size to well over 3MB. The downside to this is that most controls cannot be uninstalled to free up disk space. The only way to track where a control is installed is by exploring the Windows Registry, a process that is not recommended.

Registry The Registry is a central location for configuration entries, important system information, and sensitive settings. You should adjust settings in the Windows Registry only if you're sure that you know what you're doing.

It is very easy to go crazy and install all of the ActiveX controls you see at the ActiveX Component Gallery, but doing so could result in a waste of your time. Many of the controls that are listed at this site have very specific uses, which the average user will never need in a Web page. Read the control descriptions carefully before deciding to download them onto your system.

SECURITY CONCERNS

You will be happy to know that all of the controls that are available for downloading from the ActiveX Control Gallery have been deemed "safe" by Microsoft. There are hundreds of ActiveX controls available from the Internet today, but only those that have a digital ID and a Software Publisher's certificate from a Certificate Authority are displayed in the Gallery. Figure 18.2 shows proof of a safe control that has displayed its security certificate in Internet Explorer. If you do not see a security certificate when downloading an ActiveX control, you should be wary of its content. The control has not been verified as safe and can do possible harm to your computer.

To obtain these credentials, a software publisher must first apply for an Individual or a Commercial Software Publisher ID through Verisign at **http://digitalid.verisign.com/**. A process of verifying the company's history and financial status must be completed before a Digital ID certificate can be issued. The process of obtaining a Digital ID takes about a week to complete, and the software developer is notified when the ID and a unique key have been issued.

FIGURE 18.2 Only ActiveX controls accompanied by a security certificate are safe to download from the Internet.

Verisign The Verisign company is known as the most trusted source from which to obtain a digital ID and other items for secure communication and online commerce.

After obtaining a Digital ID, the software developer has to download the ActiveX Software Development Kit (SDK) located at **http://www.microsoft.com/intdev/sdk/sdk.htm**. Tools are included with the SDK that allow the developer to enter his or her digital ID and key to begin signing his or her software components. When the key and ID have been entered successfully, a digital security certificate is issued and the developer can begin signing his or her code.

To insure your computer's safety when downloading new ActiveX controls, the software developer's digital certificate will be displayed within your browser before the control is actually downloaded. At that point, you have a choice whether or not to download the component.

What about viruses? Though an ActiveX file might be considered safe to use on your computer, it is not necessarily virus free. A reputable software developer will not purposely infect files with a virus, but accidents do happen. Always have a virus scanner running on your computer and shy away from downloading content that you're not familiar with.

If you don't see a certificate appear when you attempt to download a new control, your Internet Explorer security settings are probably not set correctly. To check the level of security your browser is set at, follow these steps:

1. Click View, Options. The Options window will open.
2. Click the Security tab, then choose Safety Level. The Safety Level window will appear.
3. Click High to ensure that your copy of Internet Explorer is using the highest level of security. Click OK to close the window. Click OK again to exit the Options window.

Shortcut to the Open Window Type CTRL+O to quickly access the Open window.

Though downloading files from the Internet can be an intimidating task, you will increase your chances of a safer download by only downloading controls that have been digitally signed. For more information about registering ActiveX controls, point your

Web browser to **http://www.microsoft.com/intdev/security/misf8-f.htm**.

AN OVERVIEW OF THE ACTIVEX GALLERY CONTROLS

Now that you know how to download, install, and incorporate additional ActiveX controls into your Web pages, you are most likely wondering what all of the controls listed on the ActiveX Control Gallery do. If you need help using new ActiveX controls installed on your system, refer to Chapter 4, "Adding ActiveX Controls to Your Web Page."

Though we cannot list every control that appears on the site, in Table 18.1 you will find a list of some of the most useful ActiveX controls available today.

TABLE 18.1 ADDITIONAL ACTIVEX CONTROLS

CONTROL NAME	COMPANY NAME	FUNCTION
Surround Video	Black Diamond Consulting, Inc.	Allows you to incorporate panoramic images into your Web site, allowing users to scroll 360 degrees to view landscapes and other large photographs.
Citrix Win Frame	ICA ControlCitrix Systems, Inc.	Provides remote administration capabilities for many Windows programs running the WinFrame server from across the Internet.

continues

TABLE 18.1 CONTINUED

CONTROL NAME	COMPANY NAME	FUNCTION
Look@Me	Farallon Communications Inc.	Allows you to view another computer user's screen who is also using Look@Me across the Internet.
ImageKnife	Media Architects Inc.	Provides the ability to display a wide range of graphic formats within the control and has many display filters.
MediaKnife	Media Architects Inc.	Allows you to display complex multimedia presentations and applications within Internet Explorer.
Menu	Microsoft	Gives you the ability to create complex menu systems in your Web page that look like Windows application menus.
Popup Window	Microsoft	Displays HTML documents in a pop-up window, like tooltips in a Windows application.

TABLE 18.1 CONTINUED

CONTROL NAME	COMPANY NAME	FUNCTION
Stock Ticker	Microsoft	Displays continuously changing data through the use of XRT files.
Sax Canvas Control	Sax Software Corporation	Allows drawing on an online canvas through the use of VBScript or JavaScript code.
ChartFX	Software FX, Inc.	Gives you the power to create complex charts on-the-fly through data presented in VBScript or JavaScript.
ASAP Webshow	Software Publishing Corporation	Allows users to download, view, and print online presentations created with WordPower presentation software.
Visual 3Space Control	Template Graphics Software, Inc.	Displays complex 3D VRML worlds.
Sizzler	Totally Hip Software	Provides streamed animation files to end users.
Dial Control	ProtoView	Displays a circular

continues

TABLE 18.1 CONTINUED

CONTROL NAME	COMPANY NAME	FUNCTION
	Development Co.	graphic control that can be used to adjust settings like a scroll bar.
Percent Bar Control	ProtoView Development Co.	Displays a graphical percent bar that can be used to show progress in a Web page.
TreeView Control	ProtoView Development Co.	Displays a list box with data that is displayed in a tree hierarchy on many levels.
NetList	DameWare Development	Used to access network resources on a Lan or across the Internet.

Before you begin wildly downloading a huge number of ActiveX controls and incorporating them into your Web pages, you must realize that many of these controls are not free. Many software developers spend hours and hours developing these controls and expect to be paid for their time. Some controls are inexpensive, and others can cost hundreds of dollars to use. You will not, however, be charged for downloading sample controls. Most of the fee-based controls have been crippled in some way so that you cannot fully use them in your Web pages.

What does crippled mean?!? Generally, an ActiveX control that costs money to purchase will be limited in its functionality. A message might appear on a user's screen stating that he or she has not registered the control, or the control might not work on another person's machine at all.

In this lesson, you learned how to download additional ActiveX controls. You also learned what controls are available on the ActiveX Control Gallery. In the next lesson, you will learn where to look for more information about ActiveX, the Control Pad, and Web site authoring.

LESSON 19

Obtaining Additional ActiveX Resources

In this lesson, you will learn how to gain further information about ActiveX technologies and the ActiveX Control Pad.

Microsoft's Site Builder Network

Perhaps the greatest source of information regarding ActiveX controls and the ActiveX Control Pad can be found at Microsoft's Site Builder Network Web site. To enter the Web site, point your Web browser to **http://www.microsoft.com/sitebuilder/**. The Site Builder Network home page, shown in Figure 19.1, contains a wealth of information about ActiveX controls, as well as news, tools, and tips regarding Internet development.

The Site Builder Network is broken down into six major sections, which are defined in Table 19.1. Click the Site Builder Network graphic to access all six divisions of the Web site.

Table 19.1 The Site Builder Network Areas

Area Name	Content
Authoring/Editing	HTML reference guides, sample Web pages, tutorials, and authoring tools
Design/Creative	Design techniques, information about graphics, and streamlining techniques
Programming	ActiveX controls, server applications, database access, and developer information on Internet applications

AREA NAME	CONTENT
Site Administration	Demonstrations on administration, security issues, Web servers, and hardware information
Planning/Production	Strategic planning of Web sites, marketing information, cost analysis of Internet uses, and products for site building
Web Gallery	Information about True Type Fonts, Style Sheets, Java Applets, ActiveX Controls, and freely downloadable Web graphics and sounds

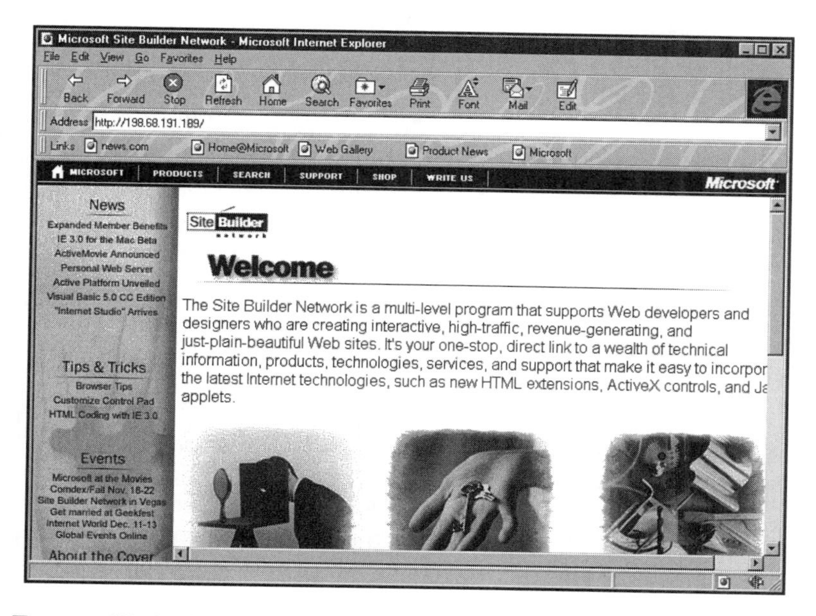

FIGURE 19.1 Microsoft's Site Builder Network is an invaluable resource when it comes to ActiveX technologies.

The Web Gallery link provides one-click access to the ActiveX Component Gallery where many ActiveX controls can be downloaded. There is also a link to the ActiveX Programming Reference, shown in Figure 19.2, which contains valuable information about controlling the parameters, events, and actions of ActiveX controls.

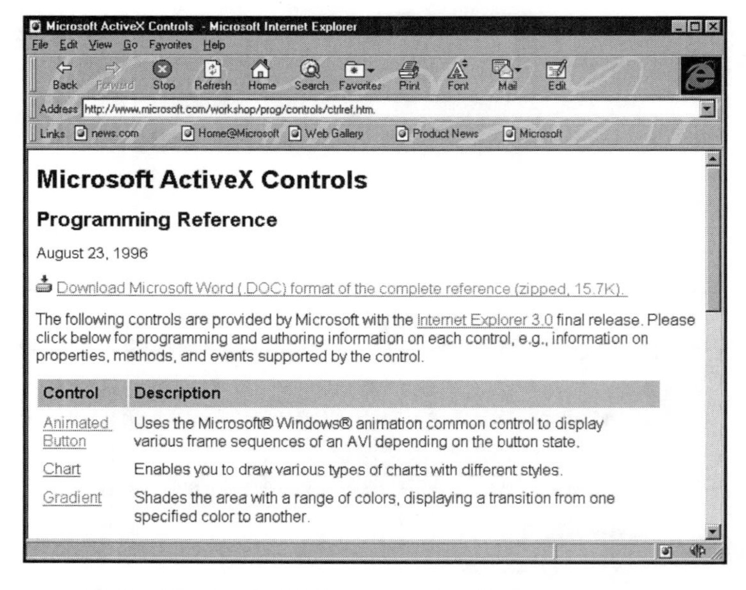

FIGURE 19.2 The ActiveX Programming Reference page provides a wealth of information regarding scripting syntax.

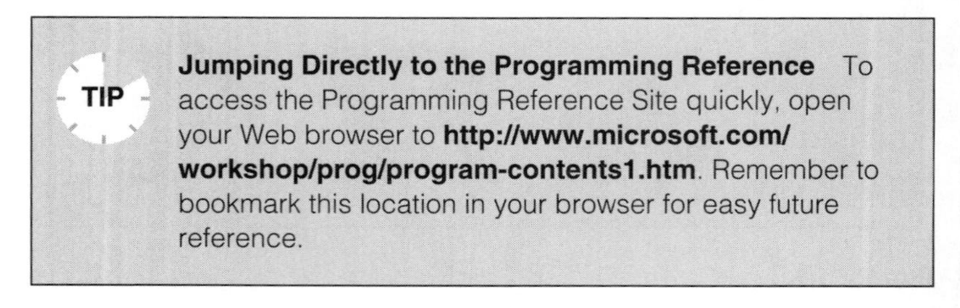

TIP

Jumping Directly to the Programming Reference To access the Programming Reference Site quickly, open your Web browser to **http://www.microsoft.com/workshop/prog/program-contents1.htm**. Remember to bookmark this location in your browser for easy future reference.

The Programming section of the Site Builder Network also contains quite a bit of information relating to ActiveX controls. You will find information about the ActiveX SDK, Signing controls, Active Movie, and FAQ files here.

SDK—Software Development Kit If you become a member of the Site Builder Network, you will have access to over 30 Internet development tools and beta releases of upcoming software. To qualify for membership in the Site Builder Network, you must meet one of the following qualifications:

- Place a button representing Internet Explorer and a link to the IE Web site on your Web page. This qualifies you for Level 1 membership which entitles you to a wealth of Internet development tools that can be downloaded for free.
- Insert an ActiveX control into your Web site. This will qualify you for Level 2 membership. Level 2 membership grants you the same benefits as Level 1, with the addition of a free CD-ROM containing all of the software available for downloading.
- Deploying three Web sites that make heavy use of ActiveX controls, and paying an annual fee, qualifies you for Level 3 membership. Level 3 membership allows you free technical support from Microsoft regarding Web site development, a free subscription to the Microsoft Developer Network Enterprise CD-ROM, and member-only conferences and seminars.

For a detailed explanation of the benefits offered to registered members, open **http://198.68.191.189/program/** in your Web browser.

USENET NEWSGROUPS

Microsoft has made a public USENET news server available for users to collaborate with other ActiveX developers and software users. The address for the Microsoft news server is **msnews.microsoft.com**. To access the news server, follow these steps:

1. Open your USENET newsreader application.
2. Open the server configuration screen and type **msnews.microsoft.com** as the default server. (If your news program allows more than one server, just add it to the list.)
3. Retrieve the list of active newsgroups from Microsoft. The list of newsgroups available will appear in your newsreader after downloading.
4. In the list of newsgroups, highlight the group you want to subscribe to and choose Subscribe. After subscribing, you can read and post articles as you wish.

There are 27 newsgroups dedicated to ActiveX Controls and programming at the time of this writing. All of these groups are updated daily with input from ActiveX programmers from around the world sharing ideas, complaints, and advice. To quickly find the newsgroup that fits your needs, point your Web browser to **http://www.microsoft.com/support/news/**. Here you will be able to select a newsgroup topic from a drop-down list and access the newsgroup from a Web hyperlink.

To help you decide which groups you will benefit from reading the most, some of them are summarized in Table 19.2

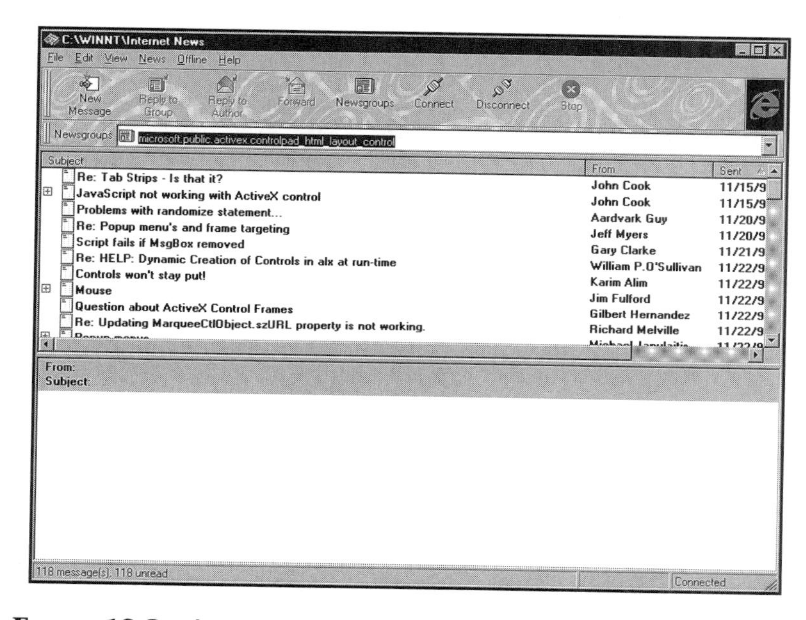

FIGURE 19.3 Accessing USENET newsgroups is a great way of gaining information about ActiveX.

TABLE 19.2 ACTIVEX USENET NEWSGROUPS

NEWSGROUP NAME	TOPIC COVERED
Microsoft.public.activex.controlpad_html_layout control	HTML Layout with the ActiveX Control Pad
Microsoft.public.activex.controls.activemovie	Using the Activemovie ActiveX control
Microsoft.public.activex.controls.usage	General ActiveX control and programming information

continues

TABLE 19.2 CONTINUED

NEWSGROUP NAME	TOPIC COVERED
Microsoft.public.activex.istudio	Designing Web pages and incorporating ActiveX controls with Visual InterDev
Microsoft.public.activex.programming.control.safety	Security concerns about ActiveX controls
Microsoft.public.activex.programming.scripting.engines	Scripting engines and implementing ActiveX controls through scripting
Microsoft.public.activex.programming.scripting.jscript	JScript language and ActiveX control usage
Microsoft.public.activex.programming.scripting.vbscript	VBScripit language and ActiveX control usage
Microsoft.public.vb.controls.creation	Information about designing your own ActiveX controls with Visual Basic

There are also many other USENET newsgroups you can access from your local Internet Service Provider that cover a wide range of information from Web programming to authoring HTML. Ask your service provider or network administrator how you can access these groups.

ACTIVEX WEB SITES

There are new Web sites dedicated to ActiveX popping up all the time. Many of these Web sites provide sample applications, programming tips, and news about ActiveX technologies.

A collection of some of the best ActiveX Web sites are listed in Table 19.3.

TABLE 19.3 ACTIVEX WEB SITES

SITE NAME	SITE URL	CONTENTS
ActiveX Working Group	**http://www.activex.org**	Responsible for the open ActiveX specifications on multiple operating systems and computer platforms
ACTIVEX.COM	**http://www.activex.com/**	Produced by Clnet, this Web site has multimedia sections, programming areas, sample applications, and news about ActiveX Controls.
ActiveX Arena!	**http://browserwatch.iworld.com/activex.html**	Form design advice, VRML, multimedia authoring, and graphics programming
Yahoo!	**http://www.yahoo.com/Computers and Internet/Operating Systems/Microsoft Windows/Windows95/Technical/ActiveX/**	Contains links to ActiveX, ActiveX games, user groups, and controls in general

continues

TABLE 19.3 CONTINUED

SITE NAME	SITE URL	CONTENTS
ZD Net	**http://www5.zdnet.com/zdwebcat/content/megasource/activex/activex.html**	Tools, references, ActiveX Files, and news about ActiveX
ActiveXpress	**http://www.techweb.com/activexpress/**	About ActiveX technologies, control database

No matter how you learn about ActiveX, the best way to approach it is through experimentation. You cannot harm anything by experimenting with ActiveX controls, and with a little practice, you'll be developing complex applications in no time.

In this lesson you learned where to go for additional references regarding ActiveX controls, including the Site Builder Network, USENET newsgroups, and ActiveX Web sites.

INDEX

SYMBOLS

A

B

C

D

E

F

G

H

I

J-K

L

M

N

O

P

R

S

T

U-V

W-Z

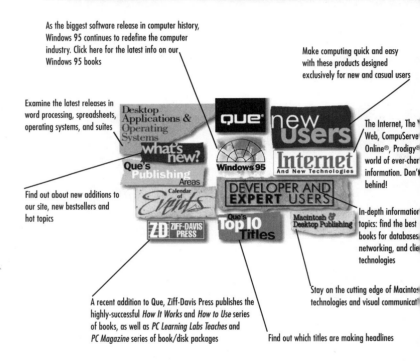